B to B BACK TO BASICS

A Practitioner's Guide to

Operations
Excellence

WITHDRAWN

DOUGLAS
SUTTON

BACK TO BASICS: A PRACTITIONER'S GUIDE TO OPERATIONS EXCELLENCE.

Copyright © 2012 by Douglas Sutton. All rights reserved.

Operations Excellence Services, LLC
P.O. Box 54739, Cincinnati, Ohio 45254

Operations Excellence Services books may be purchased for educational, business, or sales promotional use. For information, please write:

Operations Excellence Services, LLC
P.O. Box 54739, Cincinnati, Ohio 45254

Visit Operations Excellence Services online at **www.opexsvs.com**.

FIRST EDITION

Designed by B-books, Ltd.

ISBN 978-0-578-07543-3

Photography credits: Page v: © Martin Barraud/Iconica/Getty Images, © iStockphoto.com/nullplus, © Ben Bloom/Stone/Getty Images, © iStockphoto.com/Chris Schmidt, © ColorBlind Images/Blend Images/Getty Images, © Flying Colours Ltd/Photodisc/Jupiterimages, © iStockphoto.com/Leontura, © iStockphoto.com/Joshua Hodge Photography; Page 2: © iStockphoto.com/Maciej Noskowski; Pages 6–7: © iStockphoto.com/Joshua Hodge Photography; Pages 10–11: © Martin Barraud/Iconica/Getty Images; Page 12: © Andersen Ross/Brand X Pictures/Jupiterimages; Page 14: © iStockphoto.com/Amriphoto; Page 16: © iStockphoto.com/Cliff Parnell; Page 18: © iStockphoto.com/diego cervo; Page 19: © iStockphoto.com/Steve Cole, © iStockphoto.com/ David H. Lewis, © iStockphoto.com/nullplus; Page 30: © iStockphoto.com/Jacob Wackerhausen; Page 32: © iStockphoto.com/Eric Hood; Pages 38–39: © iStockphoto.com/Pali Rao; Page 44: © iStockphoto.com/ nicole waring; Page 47: © Ben Bloom/Stone/Getty Images; Page 54: © iStockphoto.com/VM; Pages 56–57: © iStockphoto.com/Lise Gagne; Page 62: © iStockphoto.com/Jacob Wackerhausen; Pages 68–69: © iStockphoto.com/Lisa F. Young; Page 74: Courtesy of Peter Mangan; Page 76: © Eric Audras/PhotoAlto Agency RF Collections/Getty Images; Page 86: © iStockphoto.com/Claudia Dewald; Page 90: © iStockphoto.com/ Maxim Tupikov; Page 93: © mm-images/Alamy; Page 94: © iStockphoto.com/Susan Trigg, © iStockphoto.com/ Pavel Konovalov, © iStockphoto.com/winterling, © iStockphoto.com/Corey Sundahl, © iStockphoto.com/ Arda Guldogan, © iStockphoto.com/DNY59, © iStockphoto.com/JoeLena, © iStockphoto.com/foto-ruhrgebiet, © iStockphoto.com/Krzysiek_z_poczty, © iStockphoto.com/Ayaaz Rattansi; Page 97: © Seizo Terasaki/Taxi Japan/Getty Images; Page 100: © Louie Psihoyos/Science Faction/Corbis; Page 103: © ColorBlind Images/Blend Images/Getty Images; Page 114: © iStockphoto.com/paul kline; Pages 118–119: © Rubberball/Mark Andersen/ Jupiterimages; Page 120: © iStockphoto.com/gerenme; Page 124: © Flying Colours Ltd/Photodisc/Jupiterimages; Page 129: © iStockphoto.com/David H. Lewis; Page 133: © iStockphoto.com/Chris Schmidt; Page 136: © iStockphoto.com/Skip O'Donnell; Page 145: © iStockphoto.com/Alexandr Mitiuc; Page 152: © iStockphoto.com/ Kristian Peetz; Page 159: Courtesy of Douglas Sutton; Page 160: Courtesy of Douglas Sutton; Page 163: © iStockphoto.com/Andresr; Front Cover and Design: © iStockphoto.com/Focalexus, © iStockphoto.com/ Grafissimo, © iStockphoto.com/Pavel Khorenyan, © iStockphoto.com/Marek Mnich, © iStockphoto.com/byllwill, © iStockphoto.com/Nikada, © iStockphoto.com/Joshua Hodge Photography, © iStockphoto.com/Chepko Danil, © iStockphoto.com/centauria

Dedication

This book is dedicated to all of those engaged employees at Fidelity Wide Processing who helped turn a vision of operations excellence into a reality!

. . . . and to my wife Renee, whose unwavering love and support over the past 25 years has enabled me to pursue my passion and make this book possible. I am eternally grateful.

Acknowledgements

This book is the result of years of work in operations and the thoughts and contributions of the many people I have had the privilege to know and work with throughout my career. We learn so much from our life experiences. Because every day I've spent in operations has been filled with learning and memorable moments, I would like to acknowledge those who have had a significant impact on my discovery of the basics and the shaping of the contents of this book.

First, I want to thank Jamie Bryant of B-books, Ltd. and the many wonderful people on her team that have played important roles in the creation of this book. Thank you for your passion for teaching and learning, which has provided the creative ideas, great editing, guidance, and experienced counsel to help me put together my thoughts in a way that helps readers take away something that's useful and that they can apply immediately in their businesses or operations. That is learning at its best.

As I look back and remember where my passion for operations originated, I can't help but think of John Sullivan, director of manufacturing for Harris Corporation, RF Communications Group. John gave me not only my first chance, but also my second in the world of manufacturing. He saw something in me that I didn't, and he always challenged me in a way that brought out the best that I could be. I also have to thank Bill Sandras of Productivity Centers International, who while helping us transform the way we manufactured RF Communications products, taught me the principles of Just-In-Time and cellular manufacturing. It was my first exposure to some of the principles of operations excellence, and what I learned has stayed with me throughout my career.

Manufacturing Ray-Ban sunglasses for Bausch & Lomb and building its centers of excellence was a rewarding experience—not to mention a lot of fun. My colleagues Enrique Aldrete, Patti Baez, Don Loomis, Gerardo

Pina, Alejandro Roca, and Luis Santos of Bausch & Lomb Nuevo Laredo, Mexico, taught me that even in very challenging environments, excellence can be achieved. You simply need a vision and the desire and commitment to turn that vision into reality! To the Eyewear Division Quality organization at Bausch & Lomb, thank you for your thought leadership in developing our Total Quality Management program. You communicated principles—some of which you'll find rooted in my five basics—that I embraced and used for 16 years to drive operations excellence.

To Ed Borix, plant manager of Bausch & Lomb San Antonio, thank you for your vision and leadership and for allowing me to do what I do best simply by setting a direction. To Pete Mangan, director of operations; Bob Buckley, materials manager; and Greg Fowler, our quality manager: Thank you for the friendship and the camaraderie we shared while driving Bausch & Lomb San Antonio to the highest levels of performance possible and to its ISO9002 certification. We were a team that lived and breathed the principles of operations excellence. Simply said, we knew how to win!

My 10 years at Fidelity Wide Processing were filled with both learning and validation of the basics of operations excellence. There is a countless number of talented people who deserve credit for what was undoubtedly an extraordinary accomplishment for all.

To everyone on the front lines in Capture Services, Outbound Operations, Shareholder Publishing, and our document centers—thank you. You are the true champions! I wish to thank Bob Donelan, president of FWP, for the opportunity, for the trust he had in me that allowed me to do what I do best, and for removing some of the barriers to achieving excellence in our business. A big thanks to Kim Cummins, senior vice president of customer relationship development, for putting together one of the most effective CRD teams and one of the best customer account management processes. You truly helped us understand our customers' needs, expectations, and desires and helped us stay out in front of them on an ongoing basis. The result was the delivery of countless capabilities and services to meet their needs and the achievement of the highest levels of customer satisfaction in the history of FWP. And to all our customers and the Fidelity distribution channels, thank you for driving us to be the best we could be!

To Mike Bull, senior vice president of operations, and his great team of Capture Services leaders including Mike Ennis, Roddell McCullough, and Gregg Prebles: Thank you for having the courage to try something new and for your commitment to excellence, which revolutionized the way back-office processing is done in financial services. A special thanks to Tom Duggan, director of process engineering, who provided the expertise, guidance, and support to implement the principles of Lean and metrics-based performance management. You proved without a doubt that manufacturing principles really do work in financial services.

A special thanks to my partners in Outbound Operations. I feel very fortunate to have worked with all of you, especially Daryl Hunt, senior vice president of operations, who taught me by example the importance of leadership with a human touch. To Greg Stanley, director of materials, who demonstrated both the importance of effective management processes and the discipline needed to maintain the accurate data and information that drive predictability in performance, thank you. You've been a great partner and friend. To all of those in Outbound who called me out and opened my eyes to what I had been conditioned not to see, I thank you. You helped me learn that only through our greatest failures can we achieve true success.

I also want to thank Jim Scott, senior vice president and CIO of FWP, and his very talented team of technical experts and product managers. Your passion for developing value-add technologies and understanding of how to integrate them into our processes provided tremendous customer value and helped us achieve levels of operational performance and customer service that I believe many would say are unsurpassed in the financial service industry even today.

I'm also grateful to Linda Nourse, FWP's director of quality, and her great staff of quality engineers, including Tracey Bracke, Marilyn Germann, Paula Hays, and Karl Kahlden, among others. Linda, your leadership helped prove on a national and international level that our employees were truly engaged and committed to operations excellence! It simply doesn't get any better than that!

The development of the material presented in this book would not have been possible without the help of Greg Klem, my good friend and colleague, and a partner at Centric Consulting. Thank you, Greg, for your thought leadership, counsel, and support throughout the last 12 years—you've always challenged me to look at the big picture. You've helped me craft credible visions, develop effective transformational strategies, and communicate those strategies in a way that everyone could understand. You taught me the importance of organizational clarity.

I want to give special thanks to Grace Frisch, my good friend and colleague, for always believing in me. To Ray Attiyah, founder and chief innovation officer of Definity Partners, and to his partners John DiAgostino and Jay Kuhn, thank you! When I needed help from an organization that understood where I wanted to take Fidelity Wide Processing, you were there. Your experience and knowledge in driving operational improvement were integral in helping us develop a high performance work environment, giving us a kick-start to turn a vision of operations excellence into reality.

And finally, I want to thank my family. To my children, Ashley, Kyle, and Douglas, you are the joy of my life. You've all grown up too fast, but I'm thankful for your understanding of my long hours and times away. Watching you mature into the outstanding individuals you are, each with your own passion for excellence in the paths you have chosen, tells me that your mom and I have done some things right. And finally, to my wife Renee, there are not words to describe my gratitude for everything you have done for me while I've pursued my passion. Thank you for all the sacrifices you have made and for your never ending love and support.

Contents

Introduction

Operations is the engine of most businesses. It's the heart and soul that grinds sometimes endlessly day after day to churn out products or provide services. It's the shop floor of any manufacturer, the back office of financial services, the processing center for healthcare services, the customer call center of a company, or the working warehouse of a distribution center. It's the men and women who work behind the scenes day after day to deliver on the customer expectations that have been committed to and promised by the guys and gals in sales and marketing.

Operations come in many sizes. From the small twenty-person web design firm to the midsize 300-employee processing operation to the large corporate manufacturing and service operation that involves multiple functions, crosses multiple regions, and requires tens of thousands of employees, operations is the core of business. For example, a midsize financial services company with multiple distribution channels may require several capabilities to acquire and service its customers, while a large insurance company may require dozens of business capabilities such as underwriting, claims processing, and finance and accounting. Each capability or function within a corporation necessitates its own operation with people, processes, and technology to support the products and services that the organization provides to its customers.

Within a small business or even a large manufacturing environment, it is easy to witness an operation in action and understand how its people, processes, and technology work together to serve customers. However, operations in large corporations easily become siloed, each operation having individual strategies, goals, and objectives. Often operational lines become blurred as more and more corporations centralize their activities into managed structures. Corporate operations groups layered on top of individual business units make it even more challenging to understand the lines of authority and responsibility. It becomes increasingly difficult to discern what the operational vision is and how the various operations can, or should, work together to provide more value to the customers they serve.

Why is this important? No matter the size of their organizations, operations leaders understand that innovation and continuous improvement are essential if they want to stay competitive in the global economy. While some businesses may focus internally on reducing costs and driving process excellence, larger corporations are also under pressure to consolidate operations, automate manual activity, and relocate operational activities to lower-cost regions. Each operations leader within a large corporate environment may have his or her own approach toward improvement. This leads to inconsistency in strategy, language, and use of improvement methods across the enterprise. Ultimately, in the absence of a shared vision and a common, collaborative, enterprise-wide approach, crucial opportunities for significant value creation are lost.

Technology and innovation move ever forward, but sometimes, successful improvement methodologies that have been around for years are simply repackaged and resold as new ideas. Lean, Six Sigma, and Total Quality Management are particularly susceptible to this phenomenon. While implementations of well-designed (or well-packaged) methodologies are usually successful at first, they often falter over time. Even the soundest innovations and improvement methodologies will ultimately fail to provide sustainable improvement if the basics of operations excellence are not in place. Without a solid foundation of excellence and the discipline to maintain that excellence, every improvement program you attempt to layer onto your operation will eventually crumble.

How do I know? I'm an operations professional—an actual practitioner. I am one of many operations leaders who have worked in the trenches for years, and I've leveraged operations as a strategic competitive advantage for three very well-known, large, and profitable *Fortune* 500 companies. My career began in the high-tech industry, where I spent 10 years working for Harris Corporation, RF Communication Group, building high-frequency radio equipment. Next came seven years with Bausch & Lomb's eyewear division creating manufacturing centers of excellence, both domestically and internationally, and then 10 years developing best practices for the financial service industry at Fidelity Wide Processing (FWP), an internal service company of Fidelity Investments. After striving to develop an operations excellence approach at American International Group for three years, I launched Operations Excellence Services LLC, a firm dedicated to helping business and operations leaders in their own journeys towards excellence.

Regardless of the industry, focusing on operational excellence has produced staggering results. With the help of energized and enthusiastic employees, I have overseen the achievement of true operations excellence. We became the best of the best; delivered double-digit improvements in quality, service, and costs; realized hundreds of millions of dollars in recurring savings; and achieved high levels of customer satisfaction and loyalty with a thoroughly engaged workforce. To be sure, there were several forces at play in each company. Still, what proved to be the single most important force in creating a culture of operational excellence—the key to being the best of the best—was a focus on **the basics**.

There are two key points before we go further:

(1) *Excellence* is not *perfection.*

(2) If you don't believe you can achieve excellence, you never will!

Excellence is not *perfection*, so don't confuse the two. What I'm talking about is being the best of the best—superior to your competitors. I'm *not* talking about perfection, which is an unattainable ideal.

While running Fidelity Wide Processing, I developed an internal consulting group called Operational Excellence Services. The purpose of the group was to provide operations management skills development and business process improvement leadership across Fidelity using the same methodologies, skill sets, and competencies we had used to deliver exceptional business results in the processing center. After we completed our first three projects, I was given the opportunity to meet with one of the top executives of Fidelity to provide an overview of the group and how we were delivering value to the firm.

This executive was familiar with my work and the consulting group, but before I even began my overview, he said: "You know, I don't like the name Operational Excellence." When I inquired as to why, his response was simply, "You can never achieve excellence." Not wanting to engage in what I felt could become a difficult conversation, I said, "Okay," and continued on with the overview. My point is this: The executive held a common but potentially limiting belief. You can achieve *excellence*, but you will never achieve *perfection*. There is a difference. Take a look at Honda, UPS, Walmart, Zappos.com, and Allstate Insurance. They may not be perfect, but they are excellent at what they do!

The second point is if you don't believe you can achieve excellence, you never will! In his book *The Psychology of Achievement*, Brian Tracy describes the "Law of Belief" as a fundamental principle of success. The "Law of Belief" simply states:

> Whatever you believe with feeling becomes your reality, and even if you have beliefs that are totally inconsistent with reality, to the degree to which you believe them to be true, they will become true for you.[1]

Tracy also notes reference to this law in theological writings, including the Bible, the Koran, and the Torah. Understanding the law of belief, also known as the law of attraction, is absolutely essential to understanding the human condition. It has been written about from a variety of perspectives, and by a multitude of authors. It was addressed most recently in *The Secret* by Rhonda Byrne. Applying the law of belief in my own life has validated it for me—I'm a staunch believer and a practitioner. Quite simply, as I work to align my actions with my thoughts, my beliefs become my reality, and my vision is realized.

Why is this important? Leadership is all about the future: moving an organization from its current point to a better, more desirable destination. To do that, a leader must believe that reaching the new destination is possible, and he or she must believe it unquestioningly. I am passionate about operations excellence and building winning organizations. Because of this passion and my unquestioning belief that excellence is possible, my organizations and I have been able to develop superior operations. Unwavering belief in the possibility of excellence is important because:

→ If you don't believe excellence is achievable, you'll never achieve it.

→ If you're not relentless in your pursuit of excellence, you'll never achieve it.

→ If you work for a good company, believe you can survive on its size or the strength of the brand, and are not committed to excellence, the company will eventually fall to a competitor who is committed to excellence. (Consider General Motors if you have any doubts of that.)

This book will provide you with a framework of guidelines that, if implemented, will help you do three things:

1. Build a solid operational foundation

2. Commit to the pursuit of excellence

3. Start your journey toward achieving that excellence

My experience in operations over the past 25 years has taught me many things, one of the most important being: Keep it simple. As such, my guidelines are simple and straightforward. They apply to any business operation regardless of size or complexity. What's important to understand is that for larger businesses and corporate structures it is incumbent upon the chief operating officer to establish organizational clarity and set the direction for all operations leaders within the organization. There is always room for individuality and the entrepreneur spirit, but a direction must be set. For a vision to become reality, a shared set of strategic imperatives, supported by a common set of goals and objectives, must be established. You will learn more about what I mean in the pages that follow.

A number of authors are referenced throughout this book, and a list of suggested readings can be found on page 165. These readings have been indispensable in helping me and my organizations achieve excellence, and I believe that they will help you, too. Many of the practices and principles I have employed in leadership roles throughout my career have stemmed from the writings of these authors. I encourage you to look into these influential books. They apply directly to my guidelines and will provide you with additional insights into the effective establishment of operations excellence. Each possesses sound, practical guidance that can help leaders like you achieve greater individual and organizational success.

About the bees:

As you work through the book, you will undoubtedly notice the iconography related to bees and wonder about the connection between operations and bees. Why are bees a theme for this book? Have you ever watched bees at work? As a naturalist, I've always been awestruck by how bees go about doing what they do. Their process is instinctual yet disciplined, and it produces consistently excellent results. Although not a perfect metaphor for business, the lives of bees and the workings of a business operation have many commonalities. But more to the point, I'm simply fascinated by bees. If you stop and think about them, a comical personal anecdote about bees will surely pop into your head and lighten your day. I have a strong belief that you should enjoy what you do, and you should have fun doing it. When you allow yourself to enjoy what you do, the road to excellence feels less like a chore and more like an adventure.

Note: [1] Tracy, Brian. *The Psychology of Achievement.* Niles: Nightingale-Conant Corporation, 1990.

OPERATIONS EXCELLENCE:

A strategic focus on maximizing the value
that operations delivers to your customers.

Operations Excellence

What Does It Mean?

O perations excellence does not just happen on its own. It is a journey that everyone in a business embarks on together. After carefully charting a course, employees constantly strive to improve until they realize a level of performance that is the envy of their peers. Achieving operational excellence, becoming truly the best of the best, only occurs if people live it in their daily routine. That is, superior levels of excellence are reached only when workers realize that their individual jobs are crucial to business results. When employees do not just talk about excellence but commit themselves to it and actively engage it, they are actually choosing to work within an environment of excellence. They realize that organizational image and performance does not belong to management alone, but to each and every one of them.

But what does operations excellence actually mean? How can we tell if we are working in an environment of excellence?

In short **operations excellence means focusing strategically on maximizing the value that operations delivers to your customers**. Through strong leadership, the power of people, the use of industry best practice, and the application of value-add technologies, operations excellence enables sustained delivery of high-quality, cost-effective services and capabilities that **provide exceptional customer value**. Companies that leverage operations as a strategic competitive advantage recognize that the effectiveness of their operation plays a central role in creating and sustaining customer satisfaction and loyalty. To paraphrase Michael Tincher's *Guide to World Class Manufacturing,* some key characteristics that are evident in an environment of excellence are:

1. **An unwavering commitment to employees, their training, and their ongoing education.** Employees should be able to participate actively in running and improving the business. Studies have shown that the best companies provide workers with a number of education and training hours each year. Training should be directly applicable to employees' jobs or advancement—not simply education for education's sake or to reach a training goal. In today's competitive business environment, employee development is a long-term sustainable competitive advantage. Attracting, retaining, and developing talent are critical to excellence.

2. **A relentless pursuit of continuous improvement.** Everyone in the organization should be focused on continuously improving the business. Some business scholars call it *kaizen.* Regardless of what you call it, you must establish a balanced business performance management process to generate the data and information you need to make informed management decisions and identify areas in need of improvement. Then, with a disciplined approach to improvement, you can reinforce employee behaviors that support your strategic goals, effectively manage your processes, and deliver your products and services in a manner that consistently meets or exceeds customer expectations. Continuous improvement becomes a habit, a way of life, and part of your culture, rather than an easily forgettable program or a flavor-of-the-month campaign.

3. **Dedication to superior quality and exceptional customer service.** Excellent operations generate high levels of customer satisfaction and loyalty by being easy to do business with and by meeting and exceeding customer expectations. Superior quality and exceptional service help secure long-term, value-based relationships and build customer loyalty. This, in turn, drives growth and profits.

4. **The use of technology and innovation in a manner that integrates people with their processes to achieve positive results.** People working in all functions of your business should actively work together to understand how their processes operate end-to-end. Together they can pursue process simplification and apply value-adding technologies, which result in a highly integrated set of business processes. This leads to more efficient operations and provides the best value to your customers. Your processes need to be connected so that everyone understands the entire process, where they fit in, and what their role in ongoing success is.

B to B: Back to Basics

To achieve operations excellence, it's important to understand the basics of good operations management. Excellence requires a strong operations foundation—a sure footing—so as the business grows, the operation can flex and expand while still delivering exceptional performance. Many companies start out with a good foundation but over time lose sight of what made them effective. Changes in leadership or the pressures of growth and competition may cause companies to fall victim to flavor-of-the-month improvement campaigns and overly optimistic technology initiatives as they struggle to keep customers happy and the business moving forward. Most of these efforts fail to meet high expectations, and leadership quickly moves on to the next fix. To avoid such a cycle, foundational principles must be established, maintained, and managed with a certain level of discipline. When you achieve excellence in what you do, there is consistency in your performance and predictability in delivering on your commitments.

POINTERS

When you visit external companies to benchmark, develop supplier relationships, or address supplier issues, you may discover, unfortunately, that it is not uncommon for companies to miss some or all of the basics of effective operations management. Through my own observation I have witnessed an American snap manufacturer that could not produce a documented procedure for the manufacture or quality control of its products—even though it was a leader in the fastener industry. This company's snaps, used on Ray-Ban sunglass cases, had constant quality problems that risked tarnishing the image of the Ray-Ban brand. Similarly, a large back-office account processing operation at a financial service firm processed identical customer transactions in multiple ways and at the same time. The firm was working to move the process to India, and yet the company had no documented procedures or process management structure to pass along to the Indian subcontractor. Working conditions at one toy manufacturer were so dangerous that one spark had the potential to end the lives of over 200 young employees. As these examples show, *excellence* was not given much thought within these organizations.

One important point to remember is that the basics of operations excellence are **fundamental**. In other words, they haven't changed over time, they are not something new, and they are not revolutionary. They are so simple that you're going to say, "Hey, I know this stuff—this is easy!" Yes, it is. But it's the simplest of things that we overlook, and in many operations it's the basics that are missing. We are constantly introducing complexity into our operations environments in the interest of improving the business or utilizing the latest technological advances. We contract with expensive consultants to help us uncover errors and develop new ways of doing things. In the process, we make doing what we do difficult. It becomes difficult for our customers to do business with us, and unfortunately, it becomes difficult to do business with each other as our businesses grow. Achieving operations excellence is not rocket science:

The key to success is to keep it simple. Be disciplined in establishing and maintaining the basics!

It's easy to lose track of the basics in the hectic world of leadership. Leaders often rely on the guidance and counsel of their staffs, which they should. But if you understand human nature and know that human desires drive behavior, you recognize that at times this guidance is self-serving and not actually in the best interest of the business. When leaders abdicate responsibility for key business and investment decisions to individual executives or managers, disaster often ensues. Sometimes leaders lose sight of customers' needs and the true value of their investment decisions. Some leaders also forget that they are leading people and that the business decisions they make can have a major impact on their employees in both positive and negative ways.

Have you lost sight of the fundamentals? Your answers to the following questions will demonstrate whether you are overlooking the basics:

1. How is your company or operation performing? Is its performance getting better or worse?

2. What is your level of customer satisfaction? What about customer loyalty?

3. How satisfied and engaged are your employees?

4. Are your employees constantly firefighting?

5. Are you currently running an improvement campaign like Lean or Six Sigma? Have the results made a real, significant impact on your bottom line?

6. Are your managers delivering on their objectives? Are they focused on developing their employees, or are they consumed by projects?

7. Do your managers complain that they never have enough time to do everything they are asked to do?

8. Have your investments in technology been as valuable as you expected?

9. Are you preparing and planning to support growth in your business, or are you worried about a business downturn and how you're going to survive?

10. Do you have a clear understanding of your company's vision, and do you have a supporting operations vision toward which you are successfully moving?

11. Are you and your employees happy with your work and personal life balance?

12. Do you enjoy going to work every day? Are you having fun?

The answers to these questions should provide you with some insight into whether or not you are overlooking the basics of operations excellence. Too often, operations leaders don't take time to reflect. They get caught up in the day-to-day, consumed by problems. The foundation they've built erodes, loses stability, and the firefighting begins and escalates. Then, when faced with a *burning platform*, leaders begin to look for the quick fix.

An operations leader should not wait until he or she has a burning platform to set the operation on a direction of excellence, managed growth, and sustainable improvement. To establish a foundation that is strong and lasting, a leader must embrace the fundamentals as soon as she or he can. If you establish, maintain, and evolve this foundation, you will enjoy going to work every day, your employees will be more engaged and satisfied, and your operation will be better prepared to handle the challenges it will face over time. So what are these basics of operations excellence, and why are they important? If you asked a dozen operations professionals that question, you would probably get a dozen different answers. But all the answers boil down to five basics, which we will examine in the following pages.

The Five Basics

A tour of any company's operations will quickly reveal whether the basics of excellence are in place. Tour leaders will proudly tell you all of the positive things the company does and how it does them. They'll boast that employees are continuously focused on improving operations and satisfying customers. They'll gladly tell you about their superior quality programs, their cost reduction initiatives, and how they're implementing bleeding edge technology to stay ahead of the competition. They may even explain that constant improvement is sustainable by continuously striving for higher levels of performance. **A strong operational foundation** is critically important to operational excellence, and a company tour will make abundantly clear whether that foundation is in place.

As you can see in Figure 1.1, operations excellence is achieved through:

1. **Customers.** Meeting their needs and requirements

2. **Leadership.** Knowledgeable guidance and development

3. **People.** The effective use of employees

4. **Process and Technology.** Creating value through a focus on process and innovation

5. **Accountability.** Ensuring positive business results

Operations excellence is achieved—in order of importance—through customers, leadership, people, process and technology, and accountability. Sounds simple, doesn't it? While each of these business basics is essential, each plays a different role in the achievement of excellence. The interrelation of these basics is illustrated in Figure 1.1. Before we dive deeper into each basic, let's dip our toes in and familiarize ourselves with the structure and features of Figure 1.1 by reading brief overviews of each concept.

FIGURE 1.1 The Achievement of Operational Excellence

EXCELLENCE
LEADERSHIP

CUSTOMER SATISFACTION AND LOYALTY

PROCESS AND TECHNOLOGY

PEOPLE
High Performance Work Environment

NORMS AND VALUES
Foundation of Trust, Respect and Integrity

ACCOUNTABILITY

This model illustrates how the five basics work together. It emphasizes the elements of operations management that are most important in achieving excellence.

Customers

Customers are at the top because operations excellence begins and ends with them. You may have heard this adage before, but it's as quickly forgotten as it is learned. Because a business cannot exist without customers, everything an operation does should be focused on meeting or exceeding customers' actual—not assumed—requirements. An excellent operation should strive to listen carefully to its internal and external customers, validate their needs and expectations, and identify key measures to ensure that those needs are being met or exceeded on a consistent basis. To fulfill these requirements is to earn customer satisfaction. Customer satisfaction leads to customer loyalty.

Loyalty drives profits, promotes ongoing business growth, and ensures long-term sustainable success!

Leadership

Strong leadership is fundamental to achieving operations excellence. Leadership begins at the top, stemming from a clear understanding of the customer and the things that are important to him or her. From there, leadership flows down through the organization as leaders set the course for excellence by establishing the strong foundation of cultural values and behavioral norms upon which every employee's actions rest. Leaders must promote these norms and values empathically, must demonstrate them through their own actions, and must employ them in the directions they set for their employees. By communicating a clear and credible vision for the operation, creating a strategy to direct the journey, and developing an environment that instills in employees the desire and commitment to turn that vision from words into reality, a leader can develop an environment of trust, respect, and integrity.

It all starts with leadership with a human touch.

People

People are at the base of Figure 1.1 because they are the force behind operations excellence. Once it is achieved by your people, excellence flows back to customers in the exceptional products and services that they receive. But *people* means more than just employees doing their jobs. It means *engaged employees*. It means employees who have clear roles and responsibilities, have the tools to do their jobs well, are satisfied with their opportunities for growth and development within a safe work environment, and understand what success looks like. It means employees who are empowered through clear leadership, training, teamwork, two-way communication, and rewards and recognition for the great work that they do. Employees contribute so much more to the company when they're engaged, and the bottom line results reflect the difference.

The critical success factor for achieving real employee engagement is management effectiveness.

Process and Technology

Processes are how we get things done. We all have processes that we perform each day. These processes allow us to accomplish our work and produce the products and services we provide our customers. Your processes must be documented, understood, and managed effectively. Through continuous improvement—which can be approached many different ways—waste is removed from your processes to make them more efficient and effective. Supportive management practices such as standard operating procedures and quality assurance help manage processes and drive continuous improvement by providing the information needed to identify opportunities and sustain effective decision making. Why pay so much attention to processes?

Improved processes lead directly to improved business results!

Technology is an enabler of processes. It should be highly integrated with, and within, your process. In today's ever-changing world, technology provides the business with the means to perform processes in a high-quality, cost-effective way. It also enables customers to engage with the company more effectively. Process and technology should never be approached separately. Operations leaders understand the importance of technology as an enabler, not a driver, of excellence. You should never employ technology for technology's sake; it should be used through your processes to increase the value of your products and services for your customers.

Technology has become critical to maintaining a high-performing business and increasing customer satisfaction.

Accountability

Accountability for results—meeting the needs and expectations of your customers—is paramount to operations excellence. In Figure 1.1, the entire process by which excellence is achieved rests upon accountability. Why is this? Accountability is the factor that links people, process and technology, and results. Accountability tells you how effective you are at meeting customer requirements, how successfully you're meeting your goals and objectives, and whether you're moving in the direction toward your vision. While those judgments are ultimately made by your customers, holding

yourself and your direct reports accountable is one of the most challenging aspects of leadership in today's business world. Many managers lack the ability to provide negative feedback. Communication of poor performance is watered down to the point that employees never get a true understanding of how they are doing. This inhibits their success, and the success of the operation overall. The second temptation discussed in Patrick Lencioni's *The Five Temptations of a CEO* is "choosing popularity over accountability."[1] Many leaders and managers fall victim to this temptation, which leads to a lack of faith in leadership, mediocre employee performance, and ultimately, poor business results.

How are you measuring success and the performance of your business?

Driving operations excellence allows you to grow your organization, realize your business goals, and provide developmental opportunities for your employees. It can also be used as a ***strategic competitive advantage***. However, you can't achieve excellence on words alone—you need to establish durable, trustworthy methods. Achieving excellence can be realized tangibly through enablers and practices that support each of the five basics. They have been tried, tested, and proven over time to be fundamental to success. Throughout the pages that follow, you'll learn about these enablers and practices and how to implement them in your journey toward excellence.

THE BUZZ

→ Operations excellence means focusing strategically on maximizing the value that operations delivers to your customers. It enables sustained delivery of high-quality, cost-effective services and capabilities that provide exceptional customer value.

→ Operations excellence is a journey that everyone in a business embarks on together. Achieving it, becoming truly the best of the best, only occurs if people live it in their daily routine.

→ Some key characteristics that are evident in an environment of excellence are unwavering commitment to employees, relentless pursuit of continuous improvement, dedication to superior quality and exceptional customer service, and use of technology and innovation in a manner that integrates people with their processes to achieve positive results.

→ The basics of operations excellence are fundamental. They haven't changed over time, they are not something new, and they are certainly not revolutionary. It's the simplest of things that we overlook, and in many operations it's the basics that are missing. The key to success is to keep it simple.

→ Operational excellence is achieved through customers, leadership, people, process and technology, and accountability. Though each of these business basics is essential, they are listed in order of importance to operations excellence.

→ Driving operations excellence allows you to grow your organization, realize your business goals, and provide developmental opportunities for your employees. It can also be used as a *strategic competitive advantage.*

Note: [1] Lencioni, Patrick. *The Five Temptations of a CEO.* San Francisco: Jossey-Bass, Inc., 1998.

CUSTOMERS:

Everything you do to drive operations
excellence, you do on behalf of your customers.

Customers

Without Them, There's No Us

2

Customers are at the top of the operations excellence model because that's where they belong—they are the reason your operation exists! Everything you do to drive operations excellence, you do on behalf of your customers. In *The Customer Rules*, C. Britt Beemer and Robert L. Shook advise, "Unless the customer is the focal point of all its activities, a company is headed in the wrong direction."[1] Belief in the importance of the customer must start at the top and permeate down through the organization until it reaches each leader and all of his or her employees. Leaders and their entire organizations must know, understand, and listen to their customers. According to Beemer and Shook, everyone in the company has the same job: serving the customer. Do your employees know and understand this?

In 2008, C. Britt Beemer, founder and CEO of America's Research Group (ARG), conducted a survey of corporate professionals that asked, "Have you ever considered the notion that everyone has a job at your company that involves the customer?" In *The Customer Rules*, he and Shook to their own astonishment conclude that "four out of ten working Americans think that neither their nor their coworkers' jobs have anything to do with customers."[2] Can you believe that 40 percent of Americans don't think that their jobs have anything to do with customers? Where do they think their company gets the money to pay them? Every employee must realize that his or her job depends on customers!

To understand how ARG's beliefs about customer importance developed, Beemer also asked in his survey, "Does your supervisor talk to you about how your personal efforts affect the customer?" Of those that responded, 51.5 percent answered "no." If these figures don't shock you, they should—especially if you're committed to operations excellence. Employees exist to serve the needs and expectations of the customer. These needs and expectations will change over time, but operations excellence will enable you to monitor and anticipate those changes. You will be able to consistently deliver on your customers' expectations and stay ahead of your competition. The basic strategy of operations excellence is to help your sales, marketing, product development, and customer service groups stay on top of what customers want, and give it to them. This is not as simple as it sounds.

As an operations leader, consider the following questions. Your answers will tell you a lot about your company's investment in customer satisfaction and loyalty.

1. Do I know who my customers are?

2. Do my employees know who their customers are?

3. Have I or any of my employees ever met our customers?

4. What are our sources for the voice of the customer? Do we get regular customer feedback, data, or suggestions that we share with our employees?

5. Do we take action on our customer feedback?

6. Do we have measures in place to help us understand how we are performing in relation to our customers' requirements?

7. Do we use these measures to guide our improvement and investment decisions so that we act on behalf of our customers?

8. Do we meet regularly with our customers or otherwise engage with them directly to ensure that we know how they feel about our products, services, or company?

Who Are My Customers?

Before you can understand what customers need, you must first recognize who they are. Both operations leaders and their employees should be aware of the following distinctions.

Internal and External Customers

There are typically two categories of customers: *External customers* are the end customers who rely on you to deliver the products and services they need to support their business and individual needs. *Internal customers* are the people inside your business to whom your employees provide a product, a service, information, or data. Internal customers set the requirements for the output they receive. An internal customer may be another person

POINTERS

All organizations have internal and external customers, and both types need to receive excellent service. At Fidelity Wide Processing (FWP), customers included not just the end customers of Fidelity, but also the distribution channels within Fidelity. FWP provided processing and correspondence services to Fidelity Brokerage Company, Fidelity Investments Institutional Services, Fidelity Retirement Services, and Fidelity Employer Services Company, to name a few. Those internal customers were FWP's largest, most important customers, and in many respects they were more difficult to satisfy than FWP's external customers. Because managers and employees at FWP drove themselves to satisfy the needs and expectations of their internal customers, those internal customers served as a catalyst in achieving operations excellence. This should be clear validation that customers earn the spot at the top of the model.

Operations leaders and their employees often overlook the internal customer perspective because they don't typically consider themselves as customers and suppliers within an operation. Departments and functions are sometimes siloed within a business's operation, so their respective goals never align with each other. There are quite often no objectives shared between individual functions, so functional groups never become interested in looking beyond the boundaries of their own departments to understand how they affect the processes up and downstream from them. But, as should be clear by now, serving internal customers' needs and expectations is critically important to achieving excellence.

SPRING CREEK CAMPUS

within a workgroup or the next in line on an assembly line. A subdivision that uses another subdivision's data analysis—like a financial accounting department that uses a tax department's figures—is an internal customer. An engineering department that delivers a new product design to its operation leaders is delivering to internal customers. Internal customers are the channels through which you serve your ultimate end customer.

Note that meeting the needs and expectations of internal customers is a prerequisite to meeting the needs and expectations of external (or end) customers. When employees within an organization work collaboratively to meet each other's needs, the operation runs fluidly and effectively, increasing the ability to satisfy external customer expectations exponentially.

The Customer–Supplier Relationship

Everyone in your organization (including you) must understand the duties of both the customer and the supplier because you will probably perform both of these roles at various points in a given year. If you and your employees are going to work together to achieve excellence, you must consider the valid expectations of and demands inherent in these roles. As Figure 2.1 illustrates, the customer–supplier relationship is a never-ending cycle of requirement and information sharing that ensures that expectations are met throughout the supply chain. Candid communication guarantees predictability in performance, output, and ultimately, customer satisfaction.

As *suppliers*, employees pass their work—their *output*—on to somebody else. They are responsible for determining who their customer is and what exactly his or her requirements are. They must then meet these requirements. A warehouse or inventory department that supplies materials (output) to employees on a manufacturing shop floor is a supplier. The supplier must know the type and quantities of materials needed, the timeframe in which they must be delivered, and the location to which they must be delivered. A financial services operation acts as a supplier if it provides customer account documents to customer service representatives so that they can review and approve them. The customer service representatives, acting

Figure 2.1 Customer–Supplier Relationship

Your Supplier   **Your Process**   **Your Customer**

Requirements   Requirements
& Feedback   & Feedback

This figure illustrates the relationship between the customer and the supplier.

as customers, may have specific requirements as to when new account documents must be in hand in order to be processed the same day.

As *customers*, employees are responsible for telling their suppliers exactly what they require. As needed, they must provide both positive and negative feedback to suppliers about performance and deliverance on expectations. In this way, internal customers function remarkably similarly to external ones. The more concretely that needs and expectations are defined and understood, the better the chances are that every employee will receive what he or she needs. This improves employee job performance, employee and customer satisfaction, and the end product or service for the external customer.

Employees must work together to understand how their processes work end-to-end, how their outputs affect the end product or service, and what the impact on the end customer and business results will ultimately be. Common goals and objectives that are shared end-to-end across a process and across functional business lines will help facilitate collaboration and positive results as employees work together to meet the expectations of each other and of the end customer.

Expectations and Needs

Once you know who your customers are, you can understand what they want—not what you think they should want or what they can be talked into wanting. Strengthening customer satisfaction and loyalty does not have to be a complex process if you focus on customers' basic expectations. The customer's most basic expectations are:

1. **Quality:** Customers want the companies they do business with to be painless to work with. Customers expect businesses to provide high-quality products and services that meet or exceed their expectations.

2. **Service:** Customers want exceptional service. They want their products and services delivered on time, and they want to work with people who are both knowledgeable about their products and services and genuinely interested in customer satisfaction. They expect companies to listen to their concerns, problems, and suggestions, and then take positive action on their behalves.

3. **Value:** Customers expect products and services to be competitively priced. They want companies to manage costs and remain vigilant for ways to improve their products, services, and operations to increase the value provided to customers.

A specific customer expectation is commonly referred to as a *Critical to Quality* (*CTQ*). CTQs are the spoken needs of the customer. They are also the key measurable characteristics of a product or service whose performance standards must be met to satisfy the customer.

Customers Define Quality

In order to meet customers' CTQ expectations, you must determine what customers identify as their most important wants. To do that, you need to ask them. Leadership cannot presume to know specific customer expectations without talking to the customers themselves. Their perceptions—not yours—determine what they will accept. In other words:

Customers actually define quality!

In addition to understanding your customers' existing wants, you must predict what they will want in the future. As the leader of an organization that prides itself on operations excellence, you need to follow customer trends so you can identify new needs before they develop—you have to be there first. Anticipating what customers will want in the future is as important as understanding what they want today. If you are continuously prepared to meet customers' definition of quality, customers will never feel that quality is lacking.

Identifying and Predicting Needs

In an organization focused on operations excellence, determining customer requirements is too important to be left to guesswork. It's also too important to be inflexible. To determine customer requirements effectively, you must establish active customer communication channels for listening to the voice of the customer. Common customer voice channels include customer surveys, market research, product and service feedback, and personal contacts. Customer behaviors such as product and service channel preferences, contract cancellations, and customer referrals are also critical indicators of your effectiveness in meeting your customer needs. Customer visits and operations focus groups are excellent ways for employees to gain first-hand knowledge of their customers' needs and expectations. These also provide direct feedback to employees on how they are doing. The information you gather should be reviewed carefully, analyzed, and shared with your employees. The way you react and respond to customer data and information will determine the course of your business. Every action you take in response to customer voices must be adaptable because customer requirements change constantly. What your customers want today will not necessarily be what they want next week. The world is constantly changing; innovation and new technologies drive the development of new products and services at a rapid pace. This constant change impacts customer behaviors, desires, needs, and expectations. You must adjust your products, services, and business strategies accordingly. Anybody remember Circuit City?

POINTERS

In some operations, customers are rarely talked about. When they are discussed, conversations tend to focus on complaints. "They are never satisfied, no matter what we do" is a common complaint. This is a terrible way to approach customers. Instead of idly wondering why customers aren't happy, operations leaders must actively work to identify, predict, and find creative ways to meet their needs.

Above all else, to ensure that you understand your customers' needs, you should establish a number of tactical and strategic listening posts. This will help you stay ahead of the curve, ensure that you offer the services your customers expect, and provide the value that they demand. Table 2.1 on the next page outlines some examples of strategic and tactical customer listening posts that are proven to work. For this table, the first column identifies the specific type of post, the second distinguishes the person or people who should oversee the post, and the third outlines the data obtained from the post.

TABLE 2.1

Method	Company Involvement	Data Obtained
STRATEGIC APPROACHES		
Dedicated customer teams	Customer account managers	Pulse of the end customer, strategic and tactical expectations
Regular company and customer leadership meetings with top customers	Executive and mid-management (all functions)	Pulse of the end customer, strategic and tactical expectations
Company-Sponsored Forums		
Customer advisory board	Executive management	Directional validation
Customer performance meetings	Customer account managers, business leaders, operations leaders, and product and systems leaders	Customer needs and priorities
Company leadership forums	Product and customer relationship leaders	Cross-company idea sharing
Joint strategy planning	Finance leaders and customer account managers	Customers' strategic needs
TACTICAL APPROACHES		
Semi-annual customer surveys	Customer account teams	Satisfaction levels
Focus groups	Product and relationship leaders	Product and project requirements
Tours and site visits	Customer account teams	Broadened awareness and best practice sharing

Exceeding Expectations

The customer requirements that you learn about through listening posts will tend to be unambiguous and understandable. However, customers can't always put into words everything they feel they need. This poses an obstacle for leaders striving for excellence. The requirements that customers have but cannot tell you about are called *latent requirements*. To truly satisfy the customer, you must also work to determine and satisfy latent requirements. That means you must examine the value your products and services provide on a continuous basis.

This entire discussion about the customer boils down to one key concept: Operations leaders must make a focused effort to seek out and appreciate the voice of the customer. They should strive to hear what this voice is telling them about their products, their services, and the overall effectiveness of their operation. Are the vision, mission, and strategies of your business delivering the value that your customers expect? Retaining existing customers is more profitable than acquiring new ones, so sharing customer information and feedback with employees on a routine basis is critically important.

Figure 2.2 illustrates the importance that voice of the customer has in shaping a business and its operations. A clear understanding of the customer perspective enables an operation to examine itself and its ability to satisfy customer needs and expectations. When combining the customer and overall internal perspectives with external factors like industry and technology trends and competitive threats, a business and its operation can evaluate its vision and strategy on an ongoing basis, course correcting when necessary to continue to grow the business and stay on the path towards excellence.

Figure 2.2 Importance of Understanding Multiple Perspectives

CUSTOMER PERSPECTIVE
- Overall satisfaction
- Service levels
- Ease of doing business with
- Views on cost competitiveness
- Customer business direction
- Key requirements/needs: current and future
- Opportunities to provide additional value-added services

INTERNAL PERSPECTIVE
- Definition of core capabilities/competencies
- Capability assessment: strengths and weaknesses of process, technology, organization structure, use of metrics, etc.
- High level breakdown and analysis of end-to-end processes
- Performance assessment

OTHER EXTERNAL PERSPECTIVES
- Competition
- Technology trends
- Regulatory changes/influences
- Industry trends (such as emerging products)

Operational
Excellence
in Action

Customers

Leadership

Life examples of leaders
like you.

People   Accountability

Process &
Technology

Ian's Industrial Parts → Supplying in a Recession

RECENT YEARS HAVE BEEN TOUGH for manufacturers like Ian Ingram. His company, Industrial Parts, manufactures complex mechanical components that are used in a wide variety of machines, vehicles, and other industrial applications. When the economy took a turn for the worse, many of Ian's customers felt the pinch of the recession as demand for their end products contracted dramatically around the world. Some of Ian's biggest customers in the automotive industry faced massive layoffs, dramatic cost reduction, and even bankruptcy.

The timing of the recession was particularly bad for Ian: several long-term contracts with major buyers came up for renewal in the middle of the economic crunch. As the contracts' expiration dates drew closer, Ian sent countless emails and made numerous phone calls to lock in renewals ahead of time. Yet many of the buyers continued to stall. Others told him flatly that they would not be renewing with Industrial Parts. To make matters worse, Ian began to see alarming signs from several customers still under contract. Unpaid invoices were beginning to pile up, and restocking orders called for increasingly smaller quantities of parts. As sales began to slide and cash flows began to dry up, Ian started to wonder if he might have to cut—or halt—Industrial Parts' production. What should Ian do to reconnect with his customers?

SOLUTION:

As a parts supplier to other industrial manufacturers, Ian could clearly see that the economic environment was dramatically affecting the needs of his customers and that established supplier relationships were not meeting those needs. He set up face-to-face meetings with each of his customers and asked them directly why they weren't renewing contracts or paying their invoices.

Ian discovered that many customers who refused to renew their contracts were concerned about their sales forecasts. When demand was strong, locking in long-term contracts was beneficial, but as demand fell, inventories began to build up. After listening to these customers' concerns, Ian drafted short-term contracts at customers' current rates with provisions to extend or renew the shorter contracts as demand picked up. Many customers accepted these new terms.

The customers who weren't making payments, as Ian found out, were having trouble with their cash flows. Many of these customers made their payments using short-term credit, but credit markets were getting tighter across the board. He offered these customers opportunities to renegotiate their prices and payment schedules.

Meeting with customers and discussing their various economic situations gave Ian a better understanding of his place in the market. Using this knowledge to identify shifting sales trends and adjust his production and distribution processes accordingly, the Industrial Parts' owner offered to exchange lackluster products for better-selling ones, optimized production of the parts that sold well consistently, and began to ship orders in smaller quantities to provide his buyers with the parts that they needed in the immediate term. Ian's proactive response to changing customer needs saved Industrial Parts' production and allowed it to weather the recession.

Different Customers with Different Needs

BETH BOCEK MAKES BAKED GOODS FROM SCRATCH every morning to sell in her stores. Beth's Bakery sells assorted breads and rolls, bagels, cakes, cookies, and other goodies—all made from her homemade recipes—through a network of five strategically located storefronts. Recently, a regular customer at one of Beth's stores told Beth that she had been tasked with finding a breakfast caterer for an upcoming corporate event, and she wanted Beth's Bakery to do the catering. Beth has never done catering before, but she is excited at the opportunity and confident that her bakery can pull it off with a bit of extra planning. Where should Beth start?

SOLUTION:

Beth's biggest concerns are the needs and expectations of this new customer and how they differ from those of the customers she's used to serving. Catering a corporate event is not a core competency of hers, and is in fact something she's never done before. Catering an event means altering the amount and type of baked goods that she produces, as well as her pricing structure. Beth knows that before she can agree to cater the event, she must understand and address these differences so she can make sure that all customer needs and expectations are met. She also knows that this event could serve as a pilot for a sales channel that could grow her business dramatically.

First, Beth considers scale. In addition to her usual store traffic, she will need to make sure that she has the production capacity to accommodate the event's volume. By discussing logistics with the customer and her employees, Beth decides how many baked goods she'll need to produce for the event and how best to reach that number while meeting her normal in-store demand. Beth determines that by beginning her day two hours earlier, she should be able to produce the extra goods.

Second, Beth considers the type of goods needed. She knows the number of baked goods she is serving, but she must determine what precisely to bake. Because she is catering a breakfast event, the customer will want donuts, bagels, scones, and coffee, rather than cookies or cakes and soda. Because the customer would prefer to have a full catering spread, Beth also needs to decide when and from whom to pick up goods that she doesn't normally carry: fruit, milk, and juice.

Third, Beth considers cost and price. While the customer loves Beth's special recipes, she's still looking for a reasonable and competitive price—Beth's isn't the only bakery in town. Obtaining the goods that she does not normally sell will incur extra costs. Beth researches local vendors and settles on one that will keep her acquisition costs as low as possible without sacrificing quality. With such a large order, Beth can afford to price her baked goods extremely competitively. This lowers her overall cost, making up for extra costs and providing her customer with much greater value.

Having considered these differences, Beth is confident that she can meet the needs and expectations of her new customer, even though they are substantially different from those of her usual clients. By asking questions, considering differences, and communicating with her customers, Beth can ensure satisfaction, make her new catering services successful, and ensure consistent improvement in her services.

**FELIX HAMILTON IS THE DIRECTOR OF OPERATIONS AT PIONEER PROCESS-
ING SERVICES (PPS),** an internal service company that employs 300 people. PPS provides inbound processing services for its parent company, Pioneer Bank, which recently acquired Osprey Savings & Loan, a large bank that fell on troubled times during the financial crisis. Pioneer Bank kept the Osprey name but folded its operations into its own business. As part of the acquisition, it decided to use PPS to process all of Osprey's incoming documents. PPS receives all of Pioneer's and Osprey's documents and routes them to the appropriate Pioneer or Osprey customer service group. The customer service groups set up new accounts, add data, or make changes to account features, and upload that information into Pioneer's customer account management system.

PPS has been processing Pioneer Bank's inbound mail for five years. During that time it has grown from 100 employees to 300 employees to keep up with the bank's expanding customer reach. Over the last eight months, as the company brought on Osprey's business, 75 employees have been added. Felix's organization has built a solid reputation for responding to Pioneer's customer needs quickly and providing new capabilities and services that enable the bank to grow the business and service its customers in a high-quality, effective manner. Ninety-five percent of the time, PPS is able to service its end customers the same day and process all of its incoming documents by 4 p.m. the day of receipt—a big improvement over the 65 percent same-day processing rate that it maintained three years ago.

Recently, Felix was informed by his operations manager Diane that Osprey workers have complained that they do not receive their documents in time to meet the 95 percent same-day processing goal. They complain that PPS is not meeting their expectations and is not living up to the agreements made when Osprey became part of the Pioneer family. Diane has made dozens of phone calls and sent numerous emails to correct the situation, but things have not improved. She advises Felix that Osprey just doesn't "get it" and that they are extremely difficult to work with. What should Felix do to mend relations with the newly acquired company?

SOLUTION:

This is the first time Felix's organization has had to deal with a new operations group within Pioneer. Felix recognizes that he has a new internal customer and that Osprey's expectations are just as important as Pioneer's and those of the bank's external end customers. He also knows that PPS is critical to Osprey's success, and that translates back into success for PPS and Pioneer Bank as a whole. To mend relations with their new customer, Felix and Diane schedule a face-to-face meeting with operations leaders at Osprey's facility.

The meeting reveals a lot. Felix learns that Osprey customer service reps have been flooded with customer calls since the merger, so employees who typically did processing are being pulled off to handle customer calls. Additionally, employees have found it challenging to adapt to and become proficient at new document processing procedures. Felix also learns that the newly acquired company never had to meet a same-day processing goal of 95 percent before and processors find it difficult to get all of their documents keypunched by the 4 p.m. deadline. Because Osprey processors are not used to the added pressure of a same-day processing goal, managers and employees alike are becoming frustrated and exasperated.

After the meeting, Felix and Diane realize that although they may have met Osprey's original expectations, customer expectations can change in response to shifts in the business environment. Working together, Felix, Diane, and the bank team agree that PPS will make some changes within its operation to provide Osprey documents earlier in the day so that their processors have enough time to meet their same-day processing deadlines. Felix decides to accomplish this by instituting flexible work hours at his end so that there will not be a negative impact to the business. Additionally, Diane agrees to meet monthly with the bank's operations manager to share best practices and ensure that the changes help Osprey meet its goals.

Trevor's Tech Reports → Competing Customers

TREVOR THOMPSON IS A WRITER, JOURNALIST, AND AVID FAN of all things technological. After several years working for a city newspaper, Trevor decided to start an independent business as a tech blogger. He began writing news and opinion pieces about current events in the technology sector to post on his website. Trevor's former newspaper colleague Teresa recognized an opportunity for him to generate more revenue by branching out into consulting and writing a newsletter. Trevor hired Teresa, and they formed Tech Reports by combining the advertisement-supported blog with a subscription-based newsletter and private technology-related consulting services.

While working at the newspaper, Trevor and Teresa had amassed a reliable network of industry contacts who were willing to assist Trevor by providing inside information about upcoming product releases. Those contacts, combined with Trevor and Teresa's experience as journalists, helped give Tech Reports a reputation for delivering reliable news and insider information about emerging trends. Tech Reports' reputation attracted many new customers, including a number of business clients and financial professionals who made use of Trevor's expert consulting. After a few high profile individuals announced that they employed Trevor's services, blog comments, newsletter subscriptions, and consulting bids began to pour in.

The additional business generated greater competition. Many of Trevor's clients wanted to be the first to gain Trevor's insights; being second in line simply wasn't good enough. Trevor felt pressured to deliver hot tips and breaking technology news before any other source. One day, a contact at Orange Computer told Trevor that Orange was planning to release a device that was going to change the face of technology. Trevor soon discovered that a competitor had the same information, but to satisfy his subscribers, Trevor knew he had to be the first to release the information.

Trevor quickly sent his notes to Teresa and asked her to "get it out to the customers ASAP." When he arrived at work the next morning, Trevor discovered that Teresa had posted the report to the Tech Reports blog. As a result, he received several emails from irate consulting clients who demanded to know why Trevor had posted the information publicly—for free—before letting them know about it. In addition to unhappy customers, Trevor's contact at Orange left a voicemail telling him that no one was supposed to have released the information yet, and that his report was not accurate. Where did Trevor go wrong?

SOLUTION:

Trevor has several different groups of customers, all of whom have different needs and expectations. In this example, he considered the needs of only one group—his blog readers. Trevor should have been clearer with Teresa, and his consultant clients should have been the first to receive the vital information. By putting the blog readers' needs before those of any other customers, Trevor tarnished his relationships with an employee, a number of important clients, and his contact at Orange.

Trevor's network of industry contacts is an external group of suppliers that he relies on to provide breaking news to his subscribers. In return, his reports can help create buzz and garner exposure for his contacts. In that way, Trevor's industry contacts also function as customers whose requirements include a great deal of trust. If he doesn't work to meet his contacts' needs or requirements, he could lose critical information sources. After leaking Orange's announcement, Trevor decided that he needed new standards for releasing information. He surveyed his contacts and hosted roundtables with both contacts and key clients to determine how Tech Reports could serve client needs for quality information without violating his contacts' trust or expectations.

Teresa, an internal customer, also suffered from Trevor's desire to meet subscriber demands. Trevor was in such a hurry to release the story that he failed to provide his employee with adequate resources or instructions. Until the early release of Orange Computer's information, he had done most of the interaction with his contacts himself. Afterward, Trevor decided that his writers—especially Teresa—needed better access to his contacts. By introducing her to his contacts, he made it possible for Teresa and others to contact them directly if additional information was needed. Trevor also met with his researchers and created a system of check sheets to make sure that specific jobs were documented and performed correctly, and that instructions were clearly communicated.

THE BUZZ

→ Customers are at the top of the operations excellence model because that's where they belong—they are the reason your operation exists! Everything you do to drive operations excellence, you do on behalf of your customers.

→ Customer needs and expectations will change over time, but operations excellence will enable you to monitor and anticipate those changes. You will be able to deliver on customer expectations and stay ahead of the competition.

→ There are typically two categories of customers. *External customers* are the end users who rely on you to deliver the products and services they need to support their business and individual needs. *Internal customers* are the people inside your operation or business to whom your employees provide a product, a service, information, or data.

→ As *suppliers,* employees pass their work—their *output*—on to somebody else. They are responsible for determining who their customer is and his requirements. As *customers,* employees are responsible for telling their internal suppliers exactly what they require. As needed, they must provide both positive and negative feedback to suppliers about performance and deliverance on expectations.

→ When shared end-to-end across a process and across functional business lines, common goals and objectives help facilitate collaboration and positive business results by allowing employees to work together to meet the expectations of each other and of the end customer.

→ The customer's most basic expectations are quality, service, and value. You can determine customers' needs in many ways. Above all else, you should establish a number of tactical and strategic listening posts to ensure that you understand your customers' needs.

→ Operations leaders and their entire organizations must know who their customers are, understand their needs and expectations, and listen to and take action on their feedback. They must make a focused effort to seek out and appreciate the voice of the customer and strive to hear what this voice is telling them.

Notes: [1] Beemer, C. Britt, and Robert L. Shook. *The Customer Rules.* New York: McGraw-Hill, 2008; [2] Ibid.

LEADERSHIP:

Creating a culture of excellence and
being relentless in the pursuit of it.

Leadership

3

Unquestionably, achieving operational excellence takes leadership. Good leadership begins at the top and flows down through the organization, creating cultural values and behavioral norms that form the foundation for excellence. Although behavioral norms vary from company to company, certain fundamental norms reverberate with nearly every operations leader:

→ The customer must be valued.

→ Employees are the company's greatest asset.

→ The company must play a role in the community.

→ Shareholders' interests must be protected.

→ The reputation of the business must be upheld.

Although these norms address different aspects of business, they all share a common set of foundational values that leaders must embrace: trust, respect, and integrity. A leader's integrity must be ironclad and based on high ethical standards. Simply put, **good leaders do the right thing!** The old adage regarding thought, words, and action rings true, and leaders must maintain consistency in all three. Leaders must also remember they are leading *people*. People have feelings, a fact that's often overlooked. Lack of emotional intelligence—insensitivity to people's feelings, needs, and desires—is an inhibitor to operational excellence. There is need for a human touch in leadership.

Leadership: Creating a vision for the future and nurturing an environment that instills in everyone the desire and commitment to transform the vision into reality.

The vice president of administration for Toyota Boshoku Corporation once described Toyota's relentless pursuit of excellence as being focused on "better, better, better." According to the vice president:

> Toyota is constantly looking at how to do better, regardless of how well we are doing. It is ingrained in the culture. A supervisor recently touted the success of his operation running at 100 percent productivity. He was very proud of what his team had accomplished. His manager, on the other hand, was concerned. "The line wasn't designed to run at 100 percent. There must be something wrong," he exclaimed. A clear example of Toyota's relentless pursuit of excellence.

It might seem like the perception of never being satisfied would have a negative impact on employee morale, and indeed, the VP confided that at times that was a concern, especially with new hires. But once the concept of excellence—being the best of the best—is internalized and employees understand that they should question everything and continually strive to improve, their thought processes change. It's a cultural shift. So how can a manager help employees internalize the concept of excellence? One must examine the concept of **leadership** and review the basics of what effective leaders do to drive operations excellence.

Organizational Clarity

Effective leaders make sure that employees understand where they are going and how they are going to get there. They also ensure that everyone knows the business and how to help the business be successful. To lead effectively is to create unity through clarity!

In *The Four Obsessions of an Extraordinary Executive,* Patrick Lencioni stresses that leaders need to create organizational clarity:

Organizational clarity is not merely about choosing the right words to describe a company's mission, strategy, or values; it is about agreeing on the fundamental concepts that drive it.[1]

To lay the foundation for excellence, leadership must be crystal clear about 12 key points:

1. The business we are in and the customers we serve

2. The organization's purpose—*our mission*

3. The direction we are headed—*our vision*

4. How we plan to get there—*our strategy*

5. Our fundamental values, or rules of conduct

6. Our competitors

7. How we are different or unique

8. Our goals and objectives

9. How we are organized and structured

10. Our individual roles and responsibilities

11. How we will measure success

12. How we will hold ourselves accountable

Communication

Effective leaders over-communicate to provide organizational clarity. There should be clarity in direct words and actions, company communication channels, performance management practices, hiring and firing practices, and rewards and recognition programs. Communicating organizational clarity brings people together and fosters a common understanding of the business. Employees learn how to achieve excellence and how they fit in on the journey. Clear communication also keeps everyone informed of issues, challenges, and progress.

Communication happens not only from the top-down. *External communication* occurs between employees and customers, vendors, suppliers, and the community. *Lateral communication* occurs between employees either upstream and downstream in a process, with similar jobs but in different locations, or at similar levels and at the same location. *Bottom-up communication* occurs when leaders allow employees to voice opinions in day-to-day operations. In order to make effective decisions, management needs to consider employee insight, experience, and expertise. Employee inputs provide valuable perspectives for fact-based decision making.

Some company communication channels used by effective leaders are:

1. Weekly staff meetings with leadership teams
2. Quarterly strategic planning meetings with leadership teams
3. Company newsletters
4. Company websites
5. Quarterly town hall meetings with employees
6. Semiannual all-employee meetings
7. Annual all-employee meetings
8. Breakfast or lunch meetings with small groups of employees
9. Employee focus groups regarding specific topics
10. Direct communication with employees during work hours

POINTERS

At Fidelity Wide Processing, leadership teams and employees gathered at semiannual meetings to share information about the operation's performance against annual goals and objectives. At one point during each meeting, employees had an opportunity to share how they were working together to improve the business. Typically, three or four teams of employees made presentations outlining the improvement initiatives they were working on and the results they had achieved. The employees were very creative—many used skits, videos, or PowerPoint presentations to communicate their results and keep the audience engaged.

Because FWP was an organization of more than 1,000 employees who operated in shifts throughout the day, we conducted our semiannual meetings in sessions with 200 to 300 employees at a time. Circular tables sat 10 to 12 employees each—as at a wedding reception. At the end of each session, we administered a multiple-choice test to see what employees had learned, with prizes for the three highest-scoring tables. Working as teams, tables had 30 seconds to answer each question, and results were tabulated and displayed on a screen in real time. When the answer to each question was announced, shrieks of delight and moans of disappointment filled the room. In short, the response to this novel approach was simply amazing. Effective communication was fostered, everyone had fun, and a strong sense of camaraderie was created. If you want to see truly engaged employees, challenge them to a competition!

Vision, Mission, and Strategy

It's always important to consider *vision*, *mission*, and *strategy* as key elements of organizational clarity. In some organizations, operations and business leaders don't feel that these concepts are very important at all. They find them corny and unnecessary—a waste of time, some would say. These leaders focus primarily on growth, which is a valid endeavor, but is a statement such as "our mission is to grow the business" something your employees can rally around? Is it inspiring? Unfortunately, this statement doesn't provide any direction or guidance as to what "grow the business" means in real, quantifiable terms. It doesn't reveal how employees are actually going to grow the business or why it is important to do so. Employees want to know where their leaders are taking them, why it's important to go there, how they are going to participate, and how they can grow and develop along the journey. Rather than just doing their jobs, employees would actually like to be part of something.

Vision and Mission

An effective leader begins the journey toward organizational clarity by envisioning a clear and credible, if unquantifiable, direction for the business. The articulation of that direction is the company's vision. Based on customers' needs and expectations, your vision should be identifiable by employees as the desired end state: it should convey the organization's abstract destination as it grows and develops. The transformation of the vision into tangible terms is the birth of the mission—the concretely defined purpose of the business. The mission is the reason that your employees come to work every day and perform their duties on behalf of their customers. A 2007 ARG study revealed that only 20.9 percent of American workers are told about the company's mission statement during a job interview. With this statistic in mind, it's no surprise that only 21 percent of employees are able to recite their company's mission statement. If employees don't know the company's mission, they can't understand why they come to work every day or how their efforts serve the customer.

It is important that operations leadership creates a vision and mission that are aligned with those of the business overall. Sometimes, they are one in the same. Some leaders spend an extraordinary amount of time developing a vision and mission. They spend weeks holding off-site meetings with consultants to brainstorm and crank through details. Companies will go to great lengths to create the *stone tablets* of vision and mission. Quite frankly, all that is overkill. The development of a vision and mission can be accomplished in three to five days of hard work. **Keep it simple** . . . and stay off the golf course!

The second habit illustrated in Stephen Covey's *The Seven Habits of Highly Effective People* is to "begin with the end in mind."[2] In other words, what kind of future do you envision for yourself? What potential do you see? Where do you want to end up? Answering these questions will help you keep your end goals in mind. Have you ever booked a vacation through a travel agent? The best agents will always ask: "What is your ideal vacation?" or "What do you dream of when you think about going on this vacation?" The travel agent is asking the client to create a mental picture of the end goal.

Creating a vision and mission for your operation requires a similar thought process. In what direction are you headed, and where do you want to end up as an organization? What is your purpose as an operation? Why do you and your people come to work every day? Thorough examination of customer requirements and your operation's strengths, weaknesses, competitive vulnerabilities, and performance over the past three to five years is critical to crafting a credible vision and mission. Don't hold back—stretch yourself and your organization. Reach for the brass ring and be creative! Visions and missions should not be long or overly wordy. They should inspire your workers to head toward a new and more rewarding destination!

Strategy

After you have determined your purpose and direction, you can begin working on how you are going to get there—your strategy. This strategy will enable you to achieve your vision and carry out your mission. I've listened to countless business leaders complain about their staffs' inability to think strategically. What I've experienced however is not an inability, but a confusion about what constitutes *strategic thinking*. The term itself is a bit intimidating to some, but if leaders keep it simple, they will quickly find that their staffs actually know the strategic imperatives to success.

One way to approach the identification of your strategic imperatives is to focus on the five critical elements of operational excellence:

1. **Customer.** Examine revenue growth, customer satisfaction and loyalty data, customer feedback, and operational performance. What does this information tell you about your ability to focus on the customer? Is there a need to expand or a need to reexamine your structure? Do you have the business capabilities required to meet your customer expectations? Is bureaucracy making it increasingly difficult to do business with you? Are you providing the products and services your customers want and need? Are you addressing customer complaints and working to resolve them permanently?

2. **Leadership.** What is imperative to leadership in your organization? Is it creating a credible vision, mission, and strategic plan? Is it developing internal leaders, planning succession, ensuring organizational clarity, or holding employees accountable?

3. **People.** Where do you want to focus your efforts with respect to your employees? Is education and training, developing a high-performance work environment, management effectiveness, rewards and recognition, talent management, or simply defining clear roles and responsibilities most important?

4. **Process and Technology.** What do business results and customer feedback tell you about your processes? Are you delivering on customer expectations, or are you constantly firefighting? What can you change to improve your performance? Where do you stand relative to your competition? Are there opportunities to increase revenue, service, quality, flexibility or capacity? Can you reduce costs or speed

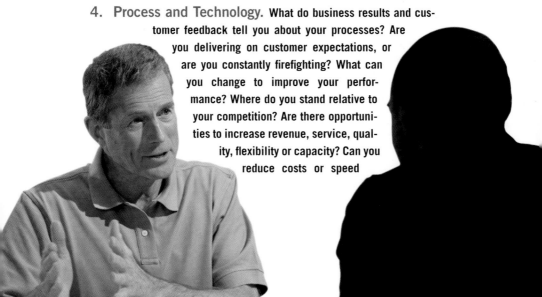

new product introductions? Is there a focus area that can create new value for your customers as well as your business overall? What innovations could help you leapfrog your competition? Do you need to upgrade your infrastructure to maximize growth? Should you improve your financial accounting systems to reduce risk and ensure regulatory compliance? What new capabilities or services do you need to be more competitive or to improve customer service?

5. **Accountability.** How are you measuring success and the performance of your business or operation? Are you meeting your customers' expectations? Do you have an engaged workforce? How are you progressing toward the achievement of your annual goals and objectives? Do you have a robust business performance management process? Do you have the information and data you need to make informed business decisions and to do effective strategic planning?

Business results, customer data, and competitive analysis are critically important to crafting a strategy that supports your vision. Don't get caught up in finding the right words. Focus on the basics, tie everything together, and provide a simple, clear message for your organization. That's the best way to create a strategy that will get you to your desired state. See Figure 3.1.

One way to bring clarity to your operation is to develop a *success model*—a key word, phrase, visual model, or symbol that defines how you will achieve your vision. Nike's "Just Do It" is an example of such a key phrase. It may seem silly to some, but such cues help employees understand where you're taking the company and how they fit in. Figure 3.2

Figure 3.1 The Development of a Successful Strategy

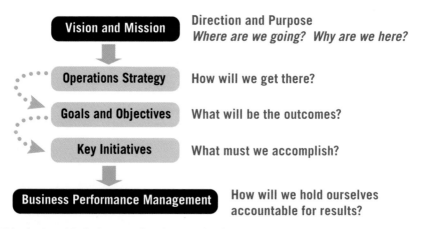

This simple and logical progression of communication provides the clarity that operations organizations seek.

Figure 3.2 The Development of an Effective Success Model

Success Model Example

Vision–Direction
To become the provider of choice for our customers, delivering innovative services and solutions that fulfill all their processing needs

Mission–Purpose
To help our customers increase market share and profitability

Customer Satisfaction and Loyalty — Loyal customers

Process and Technology — Flexible, efficient, and cost-effective processes optimized with value-add technologies

Employee Satisfaction and Loyalty — Capable, willing, and engaged employees

This example of a success model, derived from the operational excellence model, establishes a road map for the stated vision. Note the simplicity of the message and how vision, mission, and the three areas of focus tie together to provide clarity. This helps rally everyone around a common, well-understood cause.

Guiding Principles

Grow and strengthen customer relationships

Deliver innovative and high-quality services and solutions

Develop a culture of continuous improvement and strong financial management

Provide a high-performance work environment

Key Business Strategies

Increase revenue and market share by expanding our customer base globally

Improve and expand our capabilities and services to meet the dynamic needs of our customers

Increase profit margins through improved quality, process effectiveness, and reduced operating expense

Develop our employees and evolve our organizational structure to meet the needs of our customers

Customer Satisfaction and Loyalty
Net Promoter Score

Process and Technology
Quality/Service/Cost

Employee Satisfaction and Loyalty
Employee Survey

The addition of guiding principles, operational strategies, and metrics provides everyone in the organization with a clear understanding of direction and purpose, how the vision will become reality, and how success will be measured along the journey.

illustrates the development of a success model that clearly communicates the vision and mission of the operation. In this model, employees serving as the foundation leverage process and technology to achieve customer satisfaction and loyalty. The addition of guiding principles, key strategies, and metrics completes the message. Using your model, you'll be able to communicate quickly and easily how you will achieve your vision, drive customer satisfaction and loyalty, and grow your business. You will be able to demonstrate to your organization how your mission, strategies, goals, objectives, and initiatives all tie together to move the company in the direction of your vision. The key phrase, visual model, or symbol you use to bring life to your vision should be communicated through many of the employee communication channels outlined on page 36. Consistent and frequent communication must be a priority! It provides ongoing organizational clarity, which helps ensure that you and your employees stay on course toward your vision and eventually achieve operational excellence.

Goals and Objectives

With a clear understanding of the strategies necessary to achieve a vision, effective leaders can provide direction and guidance by defining goals and objectives—the key outcomes they want their organization to reach. Goals and objectives can be short-term, achievable within the operating year, for example, or long-term, achievable in three to five years. The time horizon depends on the particular goal you want to accomplish and the steps involved in accomplishing it. See Figure 3.3. Competitive threats, business risks, regulatory requirements, and stakeholder demands can weigh heavily on your goals and objectives, as well as the time frames in which you want to achieve them.

Key Initiatives

There is never a shortage of things to do in any business or in its operations. There are typically numerous initiatives or projects either under consideration or in process at any given time. A good sign that a company is working toward operations excellence is that all initiatives developed within the different functions of the business support the overall goals and objectives and help drive the organization toward its vision.

Projects require an investment of capital and resources. With this in mind, leaders and their teams should consider some key questions when assessing projects under consideration.

1. How will this effort move us toward our vision?

2. What value will this project provide our customers, and how much should we spend to realize it?

3. Which processes, capabilities, or services should receive our investment dollars? Why?

4. How good do these processes, capabilities, or services really need to be?

5. Should this investment support companywide operational needs, or should it target specific areas such as operational functions or geographic locations?

6. Are there regulatory, security, safety, or risk elements that we need to consider?

7. Whom do we hold accountable if this project fails?

To maintain alignment with the overarching business direction, leadership should ensure that projects adhere to five critical success factors. These factors ensure not only alignment but also accountability. There are many business leaders who have trouble instilling the discipline to maintain alignment but even more who have trouble holding their employees accountable

Figure 3.3 Using Key Strategies to Meet Goals and Objectives

Key Strategies	Strategic Goals and Objectives
Increase revenue and market share by expanding our customer base globally	1. Increase domestic customer base by 15% 2. Increase European customer base by 20% 3. Increase total revenue by 20%
Improve our capabilities and services to meet the dynamic needs of our customers	1. Implement image-based processing 2. Develop our web portal technology to drive customer self service
Increase profit margins through improved quality and effectiveness and reduced operational expense	1. Increase total profit by 5% 2. Achieve 98% same day processing 3. Reduce operational expenses by 20%
Develop our employees and evolve our organizational structure to meet the dynamic needs of our customers	1. Implement a talent management and development program 2. Revise our organization structure to a regional model

Using the key strategies outlined in the success model as a base, this figure illustrates strategic goals and objectives that clarify desired outcomes.

for results. The five critical success factors are:

1. All initiatives must be tied to a business strategy.

2. All initiatives must have an executive sponsor and a single owner who is accountable for success.

3. All initiatives must drive at least one of the key operating measures of the business.

4. All initiatives must have clear, quantifiable goals and objectives, a baseline for the metric(s) they are driving, and a target level of improvement to be achieved.

5. All initiatives must have a documented business case that is reviewed and approved by leadership. A post-completion audit ensures that initiative leaders met the goals and objectives of the initiative.

Some organizations refuse to adhere to these five factors, making it easy for project initiators to avoid delivering anything of real value to the business! Everyone may always be busy, but if no value is delivered, **employees are working on the wrong stuff!** Leaders who ensure that all initiatives adhere to the five critical success factors provide their employees with clear expectations and established accountability for results. Leaders themselves are provided with a preview and overview of all planned activities. They can be confident that resources and investments are focused on the initiatives that will provide the most value in moving the organization toward its vision.

Business and operation leaders sometimes get caught up in a desire to do everything. Functional leaders operating under their own agendas sometimes have difficulty separating the "nice to haves" from the "must haves." When this occurs, effort is exerted on initiatives that never deliver on expectations, are focused on the wrong thing, or do not deliver any true value to the business or its customers. **Adhering to the five critical success factors guarantees that someone is held accountable!**

If you stick to the five success factors and establish and maintain a centralized PMO to oversee all projects, you will be managing your resources effectively, ensuring that you are investing in programs that provide real value, and increasing your probability of success tenfold in no time.

During a major transformation effort for a large financial services firm, the progress of over 200 projects was documented. Absent were executive sponsors and a formal Program Management Office (PMO), and none of the initiatives were documented in a formal business case that had been reviewed and approved by senior leadership. Consequently, resources were allocated to doing "stuff." With no understanding of the investment being made, no agreement on the value the initiative would deliver, and virtually no accountability for results, no one benefited!

Accountability

Operations excellence cannot be achieved without accountability. Astute leaders understand that an effective business performance management process provides that accountability. In *Bullseye! Hitting Your Strategic Targets through High-Impact Measurement*, William A. Schiemann and John H. Lingle suggest:

> Measurement-managed companies perform better financially, an average three-year ROI of 80 percent versus an average ROI of 45 percent, and they also exhibit superior performance on a number of cultural dimensions that are likely to become increasingly important for success in the twenty-first century.[3]

The old adage "What gets measured gets done" is undeniable. It is very challenging to hold individuals within your organization accountable without a measurement process.

Business performance management will be addressed in greater detail in Chapter 6. In the meantime, as an operations leader it's important to note that a strong business performance management process is fundamental to achieving operations excellence. If designed correctly, such a process will:

1. **Establish accountability** by providing appropriate metrics to determine whether your strategies and initiatives are working, delivering on your expectations, and moving you toward your vision.

2. **Provide vital information and data,** otherwise known as business intelligence, to help manage the operation, support decision making and strategic planning, and ensure that you stay on track toward your vision.

3. **Promote visibility** of performance and customer satisfaction trends to help you respond to problems quickly.

4. **Identify opportunities** for improvement and gathering information on where to focus your resources.

5. **Evaluate the performance of your employees** to help identify developmental needs and future leaders.

6. **Enable you** to build strong relationships with your customers and employees, thus ensuring long-term satisfaction and loyalty on both ends.

Constancy of Purpose

Dr. W. Edward Deming is the American who taught the Japanese (and eventually others) about quality. Deming was a pioneer in establishing the basics of business and operations excellence. If you're interested in the origins of Total Quality Management, Six Sigma, or almost any other quality improvement methodology, simply pick up a book on Dr. Deming's 14-point management method. His approach to business excellence has influenced almost every modern business writer. In fact, you'll find evidence of Dr. Deming's influence beginning in the 1940s.

In business today, there is a propensity to cycle future business leaders through various assignments quickly in an attempt to educate and develop them. This rapid career development is meant to provide more value to the business and create successors for current leadership. The result is that temporary leaders fill critically important positions within the company. This strategy allocates too much power to leaders who have no practical experience in the functions they are leading and inhibits a company's ability to establish a strong foundation for excellence.

Being an effective operations leader requires knowledge and experience in business and process management, personnel management, and improvement methodologies. Operations leaders that lack experience tend to lead by numbers. The fundamentals of good operations management typically go unknown, misunderstood, undervalued, or completely unemployed.

You can find evidence of this failure in most industries, but service industries are particularly prone. Successful operations management, process management, personnel management, and improvement methodologies common to manufacturing industries have found their way into industries like financial services, healthcare, and government with limited success in concrete and measurable bottom line results. This is due in part to a lack of knowledge about these methods' value and how to apply them properly. Operations leaders who lack an understanding of process, have little or no experience managing employee performance in a metrics-based environment, and find it difficult to hold employees accountable for results often find it difficult to achieve exceptional levels of performance. Operations managers in these environments are also challenged by lack of understanding on how to establish measures for the processes they are responsible for within their functions. Chapter 6 will provide some insight into how leaders can overcome such challenges.

Frequent changes in leadership cause constant redirection and churn in an organization and prevents a credible vision and strategy from taking hold. The first point of Dr. Deming's 14-point method, "creating constancy of purpose," is a leadership basic that is fundamental to achieving excellence. In *The Deming Management Method*, Mary Walton writes:

> **Create constancy of purpose for continual improvement of products and service to society, allocating resources to provide for long-range needs rather that only short-term profitability, with a plan to be competitive, to stay in business, and to provide jobs.[4]**

In other words, create a goal of excellence and be relentless in your pursuit of it. Remember, achieving excellence is a journey—an evolutionary process that requires sustained commitment. Due to the competitive environment of business, you may never arrive at your destination. But you can always stay ahead of the competition. Constancy of purpose requires stable, knowledgeable leadership and consistency in the pursuit of excellence.

Operational
Excellence
→ *in Action*

Leadership

People

Life examples of leaders like you.

Process &
Technology

Customers

Accountability

Ian's
Industrial Parts → A New Way Forward

WHEN THE ECONOMY WAS STRONGER, much of Industrial Parts' growth came through sales volume. Ian always told his sales reps to go for bigger, more varied contracts. The workers in the shop filled the orders to meet the contracted delivery dates that were based on industry norms. While sales have increased slightly from the lowest point of the recession, Ian sees that the environment has changed. His most reliable customers' order volumes are not rebounding as quickly as projected, and much of the pricing pressure he experienced when he renegotiated contracts has persisted.

Because of the environmental shift, several of Ian's competitors are changing their strategies. Some have adapted their products and services to new applications and markets. Others have expanded into global markets where the economic downturn has not been as severe. While Ian understands that both options could provide potential growth opportunities, he has been focusing most of his effort on preserving existing contracts and improving market position. He hypothesizes that he has waited too long and as a latecomer into any new market will have to fight for the business his competitors have already contracted.

Ian realizes that his strategy needs to change if his business is going to stay profitable and grow, but he needs to figure out a way to be competitive. How can he remain competitive in an environment struggling to adapt after the recession?

Solution:

Ian's most immediate question is, "How are we going to remain competitive?" When he negotiated new contracts with his existing customers, he was able to stay competitive by bargaining on price and being flexible with pay schedules. He believes that pricing and operational efficiency could provide him a competitive edge in new markets as well.

To help focus on his competitive advantages, Ian develops an operational effectiveness strategy focused around three key words: *quality*, *speed*, and *efficiency*. Being sure to use these three words effectively, Ian communicates to his employees, "We're going to continue to provide quality products and services, we're going to do it faster than our competitors, and we're going to minimize waste in time, energy, and resources throughout our processes." After delivering this message to employees in person, Ian develops a company-wide communication plan to outline this strategy and its approach. Ian knows that if his company can deliver on his strategy, it will be able to outbid any competitor in any market it decides to enter and still operate profitably.

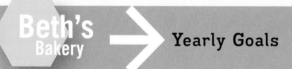

Beth's Bakery → Yearly Goals

As Beth looked over the accounts for the year, she took some time to plan what she would do to keep the business growing in the coming year. While she had conquered challenges the previous year (such as the pilot catering event), Beth foresaw new challenges for the coming year and hoped to develop a strategy to meet them.

First, food prices had been increasing gradually over the past year, and it looked as if they would continue to rise for the foreseeable future. While Beth was still able to charge a premium for her specialty goods, the increased prices had begun to eat into her margins.

Second, Beth's successful catering pilot encouraged her to consider expanding her regular services to include event catering. The pilot proved very profitable, and Beth saw a definite opportunity for growth. The prospect of utilizing the catering channel to sell baked goods seemed at once challenging and rewarding.

Looking at her situation objectively, Beth began to lay out some key strategies for the coming year as well as the strategic goals and objectives she would set to support those strategies. What strategies should she consider to help meet her goals?

Beth's first key strategy is to maintain baking costs relative to amount produced and keep margins above current levels for the next year. Because she knows that her competitors will probably have to raise prices to match increasing ingredient costs, her first goal is to raise prices on goods by no more than half the average price increase of competitors. To manage input costs, she set a second goal to secure long-term materials contracts at or below their current rates. Finally, Beth determines that the only other area in which she could manage costs would be in the production process. So she set a third goal of improving production efficiency by 10 to 15 percent.

Beth's second key strategy is to grow her business through expanded service offerings, starting with a catering service. Based on the results of the pilot event, Beth believes that she can grow her business effectively and in a manageable way by setting a target of three catering events in the first year. By limiting her new service offering to just three events, Beth will be able to internalize customer needs and expectations, learn from her mistakes, and evolve her business model to support the new business.

Pioneer
Processing

Vision for the Future

FELIX WAS INFORMED AT A RECENT MEETING WITH PIONEER BANK'S SENIOR EXECUTIVES that the company was planning to continue its strategy for growth through additional acquisitions. The financial crisis is a great opportunity for Pioneer, an extremely strong financial institution, to acquire the assets and customers of banks struggling because of the many bad loans on their balance sheets. Pioneer's CEO has issued a message to his executive leaders instructing them to be prepared for the bank's aggressive growth and for the company's ascent toward a leadership position in the financial services industry.

The CEO's message resonated with Felix. He knew that the addition of Osprey Bank as an internal customer was just the beginning and that there would be many more shake-ups to come. What should he do to prepare for and support Pioneer's growth strategy?

SOLUTION:

Felix knows that he has to create a vision for PPS around which his employees can rally. If the company is going to be prepared to support Pioneer's growth strategy, it must already be driving toward an ambitious vision. Felix starts by pulling his leadership team together to answer the key questions that will help them determine how to develop their operation and plan its strategy:

1. *What business are we in?* Pioneer Processing Services is a shared service provider for Pioneer Bank. It provides customer correspondence processing to the bank and its subsidiaries.

2. *Who are our competitors?* This is a tough question for Felix and his team, but they realize that Pioneer Bank could outsource its inbound document processing to companies that specialize in document processing. They also realize that imaged documents can be processed virtually anywhere—and as the delivery of documents through electronic means increases, so will the number of competitors.

3. *What is our mission?* To process our customers' correspondence with the highest quality, at a competitive cost, in the shortest time possible.

4. *What is our vision?* To remain Pioneer Bank's processing partner of choice by providing innovative solutions and capabilities that drive customer loyalty and business growth.

5. *What are our fundamental values, or rules of conduct?* We will work in an environment of trust and respect for each other, and we will leverage each other's knowledge, skills, and opinions to improve our operation continuously on behalf of the customers we serve.

6. *How are we different or unique?* We understand our customers and provide exceptional customer service. Although we work in a paper-based environment, we look continuously for ways to eliminate paper, reduce manual work effort, and drive a customer self-service approach. We strive to be easy to do business with!

After answering these questions, Felix and his team feel that they have a much clearer picture of where they're headed. Based on their answers to these six questions, they feel that they are ready to develop the strategy, goals, and objectives to achieve their vision, and a plan to begin communicating their direction to their employees.

Trevor's Tech Reports → What's My Job?

EARLIER THIS WEEK, TREVOR SENT AN EMAIL TO TERESA THAT ASKED if she had finished reviewing the advertising model that he had sent her. He received a short reply—"No." Moments later, a frustrated Teresa walked into Trevor's office and dropped a large stack of papers on his desk. The stack was Tech Reports' financial records, which he had left on Teresa's desk with a note asking her to double-check a few items for him.

"I've been digging through these records for the last two hours," she said, "and I'm sorry, but I'm just not an accountant. I have no idea what I'm looking for, and I have two articles I need to get up on the blog tonight. I'm wasting everyone's time looking over this stuff, and I have no idea how I'm going to fit in a second meeting to discuss our consulting services with that customer if I have to do this, too."

Weeks earlier, Trevor asked Teresa to meet with a potential new consulting client and give him a detailed explanation of the specialized services that Tech Reports could provide. Teresa obliged. The potential client asked for a second meeting, and Trevor thought that allowing Teresa to follow-up with the client would offer her an opportunity to take responsibility for a new account.

Trevor pulled up a chair for Teresa, and offered to show her what he needed her to do with the financial reports, but Teresa stared at him and said dryly, "I told you, Trevor—I'm a writer, not an accountant," and left.

The next day, Trevor called Teresa into his office. He told her that he wanted to help with her distress, but first, he wanted her to tell him what she needed. How can he prevent this level of employee confusion and dissatisfaction?

Solution:

As Trevor discovered from Teresa's outburst, he has not clearly defined Teresa's roles and responsibilities. He sees Teresa as a business partner—his go-to person for whenever he can't get something done or needs someone to double-check him. Teresa sees her position as that of a researcher, writer, and editor—not as a business partner. Many of the tasks that Trevor asks of his perceived business partner are unfamiliar to Teresa and are outside of the work she believes she was hired to do.

Trevor has a clear idea about how he hopes Teresa will progress in the business: taking on additional consulting clients, helping him double-check complex reports, and keeping the business honest while it grows. However, Trevor has not communicated anything about his business strategy to his colleague. Teresa cannot prepare for a project that she is unfamiliar with, and if she is not given time to understand her additional roles, her existing projects will suffer as she scrambles to make sense of her new work.

By discussing the situation, Trevor and Teresa began to understand their different views of Teresa's role within the firm. She came to see that Trevor wasn't just piling on extra work, but that he was offering her opportunities to advance herself and the business. Trevor was also able to see that there were some things, like accounting, that Teresa felt underqualified to do. Once each understood the other's point of view, they were able to define Teresa's future roles and responsibilities together. They identified areas in which she might be able to help (but needed further training) and established explicit areas for which she would not be responsible.

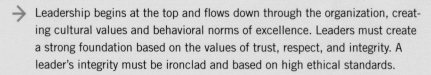

THE BUZZ

→ Leadership begins at the top and flows down through the organization, creating cultural values and behavioral norms of excellence. Leaders must create a strong foundation based on the values of trust, respect, and integrity. A leader's integrity must be ironclad and based on high ethical standards.

→ Lack of emotional intelligence—insensitivity to people's feelings, needs, and desires—is an inhibitor to operational excellence. There is need for a human touch in leadership.

→ Effective leaders overcommunicate to provide organizational clarity, which brings people together and fosters a common understanding of the business and where it's headed. Clear communication also keeps everyone informed of issues, challenges, and progress.

→ It's always important to consider vision, mission, and strategy, key elements of organizational clarity. Employees want to know where their leaders are taking them, why it's important to go there, how they are going to get there, how they are going to participate, and how they can grow and develop along the journey.

→ With a clear understanding of the strategies necessary to achieve a vision, effective leaders can provide direction and guidance by defining goals and objectives—the key outcomes they want their organization to accomplish.

→ To maintain alignment with the overarching business direction, leadership should ensure that the investments and initiatives that support their goals and objectives adhere to five critical success factors. These factors ensure not only alignment but also accountability. Accountability for results is paramount.

→ Create a goal of excellence and be relentless in your pursuit of it. You may never arrive at your destination, but you can always stay ahead of the competition. Constancy of purpose facilitates stable, knowledgeable leadership and consistency in the pursuit of excellence.

Notes: [1] Lencioni, Patrick. *The Four Obsessions of an Extraordinary Executive.* San Francisco: Jossey-Bass, Inc., 2000; [2] Covey, Stephen. *The 7 Habits of Highly Effective People.* New York: Free Press, 2004; [3] Schiemann, William A., and John H. Lingle. *Bullseye! Hitting Your Strategic Targets through High-Impact Measurement.* New York: Free Press, 2005; [4] Walton, Mary. *The Deming Management Method.* New York: Perigree Books, 1986.

PEOPLE:

A group of employees with talent, drive, and enthusiasm
to propel the organization toward excellence.

People

The Force Behind Excellence

4

Y ou may not realize it, but your people are the force that propels you toward excellence. Leaders are responsible for establishing a vision and creating an environment that breeds high performance, but it is through the talent and the power of your organization's people that operational excellence becomes a **reality**. "Our people are our greatest asset" has been a basic value at virtually every business I have worked for or visited. As a leader, ask yourself: Do I really believe this statement, or do I simply pay it lip service? If you want to know the truth, ask your employees.

Values: The Foundation

Nothing solid and lasting can be built on shaky ground. Values are the foundation of the operations excellence model, the base upon which your behaviors rest. Establishing a foundation built on the values of trust, respect, and integrity enables leaders to create a high-performance work environment. That environment, in turn, makes possible both day-to-day and long-term employee engagement; because if trust, respect, and integrity are reinforced through leaders' words and actions, they will serve as guideposts for employee behavior. There must be a constancy of purpose to maintain these values, which are absolutely fundamental to the achievement of excellence and long-term success.

Trust

Trust is difficult to earn but very easy to lose. It is fundamental to effective leadership and high-performing teams. Without trust, employees have negative thoughts about leaders, peers, and subordinates. Energy is focused more on political maneuvering and self-preservation than on the initiatives that drive the success of the business. To achieve and maintain trust, be consistent in your words and actions, preserve your integrity and strength of character, develop emotional intelligence, and build strong relationships. Trust is earned when you deliver on all your commitments, both important and inconsequential.

Respect

It is through respect for one another that our systems and institutions evolve. Effective leaders respect customers and their expectations, employees and their diverse opinions and approaches, and change, which is inevitable and should be thought of as exciting rather than excruciating. Because they better understand their people, customers, and environment, leaders who commit themselves to respectful lives will always be the first to improve the business.

Integrity

Integrity is marked by consistency, soundness, and steadfastness. It is cultivated by the maintenance of high ethical standards and doing the right thing. The Greek philosopher Aristotle argued that unethical behavior is driven by human desire, and true happiness is achieved when one lives an ethical life. It follows then that success is achieved when one does the right thing.

We have all witnessed what happens when leaders make unethical choices. Employees of Enron and Tyco, customers of Bernard Madoff's financial services firm, and U.S. taxpayers affected by the sub-prime mortgage

crisis have all suffered tremendously because of unethical business practices. The impact on the unethical leaders themselves, and worse their families, has also been catastrophic. For operations excellence to become a reality, a leadership's integrity must be ironclad.

Employee Engagement

You've probably heard the term *engagement* before. Quite frankly, many find this concept difficult to accept, or even understand, yet the effects of engagement are easy to recognize.

Engagement results in consistent and constructive action on behalf of the customer by every employee.

The important point about engagement is that it is not an action, nor is it something that you can give to people.

Employee engagement is a result!

Engagement is a challenging concept because it involves people, and any system involving people is inherently challenging. Successful engagement entails an intricately interwoven web of people who are well equipped and empowered to act. See Figure 4.1 on the next page. A leader must be able to trust every member of the web to wield his or her skills, knowledge, and authority appropriately under a common set of values. If this web of engagement is successfully woven, your people will think and act more constructively on behalf of your customers.

Engagement is not as complicated as it sounds, but it is a challenge for businesses to establish a truly engaging and high-performing work environment. The engagement model illustrated in Figure 4.2 on page 59 clarifies how the basic elements of engagement are arranged and relate to each other. In short, if employees enjoy doing what they do, are equipped with the tools, resources, and authority to act on behalf of the customer, and get recognized for their accomplishments, then they are well on their way to full engagement.

Figure 4.1 The Interwoven Web of Employee Engagement

Within an intricately interwoven web of people who are well equipped and empowered to act, people behave in positive ways.

Creating the High-Performance Work Environment

A high-performance work environment becomes a reality through a foundation of trust, respect, and integrity, and through the power of employee engagement. This high-performance work environment is one in which individual strengths are put to use where they can best serve the company and its employees. It's an environment in which employees get to do what they do best every day, in which there is organizational clarity, and in which employees work together toward common goals and objectives. It's an environment in which everyone is committed to making the company vision

Figure 4.2 The Employee Engagement Model

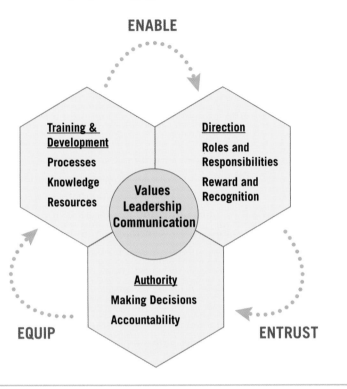

a reality, and exceptional results are delivered day after day. Does this seem unrealistic? Is it an unattainable ideal? No. As long as leadership works toward a culture based on trust, respect, and integrity and is committed to employee engagement, it will be working toward operational excellence. Operational excellence and a high-performance work environment go hand in hand.

Four key categories of excellence enablers will help you develop a high-performance work environment and achieve the positive results of an engaged workforce. These categories are management effectiveness, safety and housekeeping, teamwork, and rewards and recognition.

Management Effectiveness

Management effectiveness is often overlooked by operations leaders, even if they're pursuing operations excellence. A leader's ability to communicate organizational clarity, establish foundational values, and cultivate a high-performance work environment is severely hampered if management effectiveness is absent.

As businesses and their operations grow, leaders traditionally reward their best performers with increased responsibility, which moves them into lead management roles. In many businesses, climbing the managerial ladder is the only path to higher compensation, additional benefits, and prestige. Unfortunately, some leaders place unprepared, incapable, and begrudging individuals in managerial positions and sometimes rob their businesses of key skills and technical talent that is needed at tactical levels. In many businesses, managers gravitate toward project work because they feel more comfortable with it and get rewarded for delivering. They become so involved with specific projects that they can't devote any time to their most important responsibilities: **managing and developing their people.**

Marcus Buckingham and Curt Coffman challenge traditional beliefs about management in the book *First, Break All the Rules.* In this 1999 bestseller, they provide insights into how great managers leverage the power of their people. Utilizing in-depth interviews of more than 80,000 managers at more than 400 companies, the authors theorize that the front-line manager is the key to attracting and retaining the best employees. Because of successful front-line managers, employees deliver consistently exceptional business results.

Five Steps toward Effective Management

Every leader knows who his or her engaged employees are. They are the individuals a manager can repeatedly call upon to make things happen. They are his or her "go to" people. Imagine if you had ten times the number of these people that you have now. Imagine how much more effective you and your operation would be. If you utilize the power of management effectiveness, you can develop them. But how does one achieve management effectiveness in the real world? Study and application of Buckingham and Coffman's principles led to the development of five practical steps for doing just that.

Step One: Select Great People Simply put, **great managers surround themselves with great people.** An employee with the talent, drive, and enthusiasm to propel the organization toward excellence is an utterly invaluable resource. Finding and hiring such people is easier said than done, however. In fact, indentifying great people might be the most difficult task

Both *First, Break All the Rules* by Marcus Buckingham and Curt Coffman and *The One Thing You Need to Know* by Marcus Buckingham are exceptional resources for leaders. Each provides an expert perspective on and detailed analysis of how to develop management effectiveness within your own operation. However, simply reading and attempting to apply the concepts presented in these books is not always effective—a disciplined approach and managed execution are also critical to success. While reading these books, operational leaders should engage employees and work with them in small groups to understand the principles therein. After discussing the key concepts, leaders and employees can work together to apply them effectively. With the assistance of human resource development organizations, a leader can then implement an evaluation methodology to gage his or her managerial talent and ability to foster innovation, creativity, and exceptional business performance. Gallup Consulting's Q12© management effectiveness program is one such methodology.

Management effectiveness and employee engagement programs such as Q12© provide applicable information and data that leaders can use to drive real improvements in employee engagement. Regardless of the methodology that's utilized, constancy of purpose is critical to success. In other words, stick to it! Commitment to the program ensures that you'll be able to analyze employee information and data over an extended period of years, allowing you to determine whether your efforts are moving you in the right direction. By avoiding the temptation to jump from one methodology to another, you minimize variation and strengthen your ability to achieve your desired end state—a high-performing work environment.

that excellent managers face. *Topgrading* author and business consultant Bradford D. Smart suggests:

> Proactively seeking out and employing the most talented people can have a multiplier effect on the creation of other competitive advantages. High performers, the A players, contribute more, innovate more, work smarter, earn more trust, display more resourcefulness, take more initiative, develop better business strategies, articulate their vision more passionately, implement change more effectively, deliver higher quality work, demonstrate greater teamwork, and find ways to get the job done in less time with least cost.[1]

Hiring the best people takes time and effort. In *Topgrading*, Smart introduces the Chronological In-Depth Structured (CIDS) interview guide, which details a process for understanding the true strengths and weaknesses of candidates. Proven tools such as the CIDS interview guide increase the probability of hiring a great employee. Examine your own hiring process and ask yourself, "Am I putting the right amount of time and effort into securing the best people for my operation? Should I consider a new strategy?"

Great managers select people based on their talents. This ensures the right fit for every role. Talented individuals can be recognized by their natural abilities and the successes that they achieve. Talent is evident in great musicians such as violinist Itzhak Perlman and professional athletes such as former Arizona Cardinals quarterback Kurt Warner. Though they spent years perfecting their respective crafts, they were clearly born with unbelievable natural ability.

Great managers, however, know that talent isn't always a natural endowment—it can be cultivated. According to research presented in *First, Break All the Rules*, great managers define a talent as "a recurring pattern of thought, feeling, or behavior that can be productively applied."[2] In other words, talents are duties that can be performed often, efficiently, and effortlessly. Everyone has talents. Some are developed and used often, while others may go unrecognized. Your own unique combination of talents has been and will continue to be a consistently reliable resource throughout your life. How does a talent relate to performance?

When a role is performed by a talented employee, it is more likely to be performed excellently.

Marcus Buckingham says in *The One Thing You Need to Know* that "The job of a great manager is to identify [his or her] employee[s'] talents and figure out the best way to transform these talents into performance."[3] Indeed, it is management's responsibility to align employees with the roles and responsibilities that best match their individual talents. This is especially important during the interview process. Everyone has the ability to be a productive employee. The challenge is finding the right fit for everyone's talents. Placing employees in challenging positions that correspond with their talents motivates them to be good employees. This encourages a high-performance work environment, which in turn drives operations excellence.

Step Two: Define Roles and Responsibilities A friend changed jobs in 2008. After she had been at her new job for two weeks, I asked her, "So, how's the new job going? What are your responsibilities?" She told me that she was a technical assistant, but could not articulate the activities for which she was responsible. Her manager had told her that they would "figure it out as they go." Does this scenario sound familiar? Do you think my friend was set up for success? Do you think she was motivated? She sounded confused to me. What was missing? **Great managers establish clearly defined roles and responsibilities for each of their employees.**

Managers should produce a documented job description for each position in the organization. A survey conducted by ARG revealed that only 59.2 percent of all working Americans have a written job description. A job description outlines an employee's role, key responsibilities, expected interactions, and the talents, skills, and competencies required to perform the role successfully. Being able to provide this information for each employee is fundamental to being a great manager. Further, all employees should **expect** this from their managers. A concrete job description not only clarifies an employee's role within the business, it also promotes engagement and enables an employee to examine his or her own strengths and weaknesses. This knowledge allows employees and managers to work together to create specific and personalized development plans, which motivate workers to address and manage their weaknesses, capitalize on their strengths, and develop exponentially as workers. Simply stated, informed employees propel the organization toward excellence.

Step Three: Establish Accountability **Great managers make their performance expectations very clear.** You should communicate your expectations in concrete terms, but allow employees the freedom to achieve goals with some flexibility in methodology. Company policies and procedures must be adhered to, but great managers are always open to the opinions of their people. An allowance to innovate can be extremely motivating—even empowering—for the individual, and the discovery of a better way to achieve a desired result is certainly beneficial for the company. To ensure that experimentation never goes off track, you should establish quantifiable metrics and remain very active in the monitoring process. The best managers do not waiver. They maintain consistency in their expectations and are not afraid to confront employees on performance or behavior that is inconsistent with the company's values.

Employees must understand unequivocally how their performance is being measured and must recognize that they are accountable for achieving the goals they have agreed upon. Employees will accept accountability when they understand their roles and responsibilities. When they have been involved in establishing their objectives, have the tools and resources to accomplish their goals, and understand that it is okay to ask for help when they need it, employees will not only readily accept accountability, they will also be motivated to do exceptional work and strive to exceed expectations.

Accountability is paramount in achieving excellent results!

Managers who do not hold their people accountable make life very difficult for effective new managers coming into an organization. If employees are not accustomed to an environment of accountability, they will be less likely to accept responsibility for results. That's why it's important for every manager to learn how to have difficult conversations about poor performance with employees. It is an aspect of managing that many people fail to do, but allowing bad behavior to persist breeds an environment of entitlement and mediocrity. In such an environment, employees begin to believe that they deserve bonuses and merit increases for merely showing up for work. Habits of indifference and unaccountability, once instilled, are incredibly difficult to break.

Entitlement is a roadblock to sustained improvement and excellence!

Step Four: Educate and Develop **Great Managers know that employee development is key to maintaining a high-performance work**

environment and sustaining operational excellence. They also know that the primary responsibility for employee development lies with employees **themselves!** Managers exist to guide and assist in employee development, but employees must take responsibility for determining where it is they want to go professionally. An employee must work with his or her manager to choose a destination and develop a road map to get there. He or she should establish a personal vision, and to ensure that it is achieved, the employee should be relentless in its pursuit.

Too often, employees believe that their managers will take the lead in developing them and ensuring that they move up the ladder within the organization. Unfortunately, this is not a realistic perspective on employee development. Rather, it creates a false hope, which can lead to disappointment and frustration. Employees need to understand that they must take the initiative in their professional development, and their managers can be relied upon only for guidance and direction. To that end, great managers often encourage their employees to create development plans to manage their professional growth.

Development can take a number of forms, such as:

→ Maintaining a high-performance work environment

→ Increasing technical and professional expertise

→ Broadening capabilities by learning new skills and competencies

→ Increasing job mastery

→ Establishing more control over the work environment

→ Internalizing operations-excellence philosophies

→ Helping other individuals advance in their careers

→ Maintaining a competitive advantage in the industry at both personal and professional levels

Many companies reimburse educational expenses if they apply to the job. FWP's Rewards and Recognition program provided a monetary incentive to any employee who completed a two- or four-year college degree program that applied to his or her job or development plan. The Rewards and Recognition incentive was taken advantage of by many employees who were committed to their own development. Still, employees must understand that businesses are limited in the internal development programs they can offer. External development is available through industry seminars and conferences, professional course work at colleges and universities, and recognized professional organizations like the Association for Operations Management (APICS) and the American Society for Quality (ASQ).

Step Five: Show That You Care! Emotionally intelligent leaders understand that people—their greatest assets—have complex feelings. Consideration of employee feelings is critically important whether managing and developing people, strengthening the organization, or fostering a high-performance work environment. As you think about your operation's effectiveness, consider whether managers make their employees feel part of the operation. It is often said that employees don't leave companies—they leave managers. The manager is the employee's window into the company. It is through the manager that the employee comes to understand the company's values, vision, mission, and strategy. What messages do your managers send to your employees about your company?

To achieve excellence, leaders must create an environment in which everyone feels valued. Almost everyone has had a leader that can be admired

Leaders who are conditioned throughout their lives and careers to drive relentlessly toward their goals and always put the bottom line first sometimes have to learn to cultivate their emotional intelligences the hard way. In high-tech industries, profit margins are slim and leadership always presses its managers to push costs down, pull quality up, and bring customer service to the highest of levels. If you're not careful, you may overlook the emotional needs of your people, and they will come to resent you for it. Emotional intelligence is critical to long-term success.

As an example, an emotionally intelligent leader might walk the operations floor every morning or evening. By making him or herself visible to employees, stopping and talking with them and getting to know them on a personal level, a leader can demonstrate that he or she cares about them. This is leadership with a human touch! We all spend a tremendous amount of time at work. To create a high-performance work environment, it is fundamental for managers to get to know their people and demonstrate that they care about them. As Marcus Buckingham says in *The One Thing You Need to Know*, "Managers must convince their employees that their success is paramount."[4] Is there someone (whose name you may not know) that you pass in the hall every day and greet with "How's it going?" Do you really care how this person's day is going? Next time you pass them, stop and introduce yourself. It's not hard to do, and you may actually start a real relationship. Show that you care!

Here's another example. Company leaders at Bausch & Lomb's Eyewear Division were tasked with moving labor-intensive processes from U.S. facilities to a newly established operation in Nuevo Laredo, Mexico. Initially, 50 employees made simple Ray-Ban sunglass cases at the new plant. That changed when leadership introduced an extremely proficient and high-performing management and production team. After four years of hard work, the plant had evolved into a center of manufacturing excellence. Over 300 employees manufactured sunglass cases, frame enhancements, and injection-molded plastic frame components. The plant was so successful that it was also able to manufacture toothbrush heads and charger bases for Bausch & Lomb's Oral Care Division.

(continued)

Nearly 85 percent of the plant's employees were 16- and 17-year-old girls, many of whom had left their families to come to the border in search of work. Some owned nothing more than the clothes on their backs. The company leaders that oversaw the move were struck by the environment that the management team had created to attract and retain workers. Ongoing training and development courses were provided to each employee, as was transportation to and from the plant. Each employee received breakfast and lunch free of charge, as well as educational courses on basic hygiene and personal care. To ensure good employee health, a doctor provided full-time on-site medical services.

The work environment functioned more like a family than the rigid hierarchy you might typically experience in the United States. Each of the managers treated his or her employees extremely well. They guided and educated employees, and helped them to succeed. Whenever company leaders returned to Nuevo Laredo from a trip to the United States, they were greeted with hugs and a warm welcome. The managers, employees, and leadership all felt a sense of belonging—a feeling that became part of the heart and soul of the operation.

for his or her strength of character and appreciation of people. This is a special kind of leader—**a leader with a human touch.** During a difficult time at FWP, Mike Ennis, vice president of inbound operations, shared some thoughts about George Campbell, a senior Fidelity executive whom he considered the "best boss" he'd ever had:

> He cared. He showed it by being visible, engaging, approachable, and he always seemed to ask about family or what you were doing over the weekend, during vacation, etc. Most importantly, he was genuine and sincere. He wasn't afraid to let his hair down—he was a friend at the same time he was a boss. He enjoyed a good laugh and took the time to express himself. Everyone trusted him, and everyone felt comfortable being around him. He could be the biggest pain in the rear end at times but he always followed up to make sure he picked you up after tearing you to shreds. Most times, he wore his emotions on his sleeve. A good thing because you always knew where you stood and you knew what he stood for.

As you journey through the different stages of your career toward a destination of excellence, remember the importance of always showing that you care and maintaining a human touch.

Safety and Housekeeping: A Place for Everything; Everything in Its Place

Safety and good housekeeping are important not just to achieve operations excellence but also to improve the general well-being of your employees. The first thing that many people notice when they walk into a hospital is how clean, bright, and organized everything is. There's good reason for this: the personal safety and well-being of patients are at stake. A hospital's staff has to maintain a clean and organized work environment so it can react quickly to emergencies. Doctors and nurses must have everything they need at hand so that they can avoid contaminating the patient and possibly worsening his or her condition. Excellent hospitals are **fast, clean, and efficient.**

Achieving operations excellence is no different. If you were to visit a Toyota or Honda manufacturing plant, the first thing you'd notice would be how clean, bright, and organized everything is. It's no coincidence—Japanese manufacturers have long been known for efficient and safe operations and an understanding these start with good housekeeping. A place for everything and everything in its place make Japanese manufacturers fast, clean, and efficient.

Great leaders and managers understand that safety and good housekeeping are integral to a high-performance work environment. They commit themselves to the establishment and upkeep of a safe, clean work environment. The values, performance, and attitudes of a workforce are reflected by the company facility and the employees' work areas. This is true in both manufacturing and service industries. Make no mistake—there are no exceptions.

In March 2007, Eleazar Torres-Gomez was killed at an Oklahoma Cintas laundry plant when he was dragged into an industrial dryer. The dryer's protective guard had been removed. Cintas CEO Scott Farmer expressed remorse about the accident, saying, "Any accident is one too many at Cintas, and we remain heartbroken over the loss of our friend and partner." Later that year, a Federal

OSHA report proposed a $2.78 million penalty be levied against Cintas for 42 willful violations of its lockout/tag-out standard procedure. Additional accidents were just waiting to happen! The moral of this cautionary tale is that leaders must act responsibly when it comes to the issue of safety. This is especially true for industries in which loss of life is a potential threat. Leaders must make safety a priority and make sure that their employees understand the potential impact of an unsafe work environment.

There is no room for complacency when it comes to employee safety!

5S: The Five Pillars of a Safe, Effective Operation

An employee's life is the ultimate price to pay for unsafe working conditions. Because the consequences of an unsafe work environment are so dire, leaders and managers must make worker safety their first priority. The disciplined enforcement of safety guidelines and procedures is as important as their establishment. Leaders and managers must be aware, set the example, and show their employees that they care! There are multiple ways to approach safety and good housekeeping in your operation. Whichever path you choose, discipline in execution and adherence to policies and procedures are mandatory. A particularly effective safety program is called **5S: The Five Pillars of a Safe and Efficient Operation**. If operations professionals follow its five directives, they will establish a safer, more excellent work environment. But as Figure 4.3 illustrates, all five are needed together to achieve this goal.

The First Pillar: Sort The first pillar focuses on organization. It corresponds to a principle of just-in-time, a Toyota manufacturing technique that gained worldwide attention in the early 1980s: "Only what is needed, in the amounts needed, when needed." Organization means removing from the workplace all items that are not needed for current production, processing, or customer service. Managers should sort through company workspaces, leaving only the bare essentials needed to perform necessary tasks. In other words, **get rid of the clutter!** Clutter comes in many forms. Stacks of unprocessed reports or paper awaiting imaging may clutter an office. In manufacturing, clutter may take the form of excess materials, inventory, tooling, or old pieces of equipment sitting idle on the production floor. To quickly judge the effectiveness and organization of your people, simply look at their offices or work areas. Clutter is a good indicator of disorganization and ineffectiveness!

Figure 4.3 5S: The Five Pillars

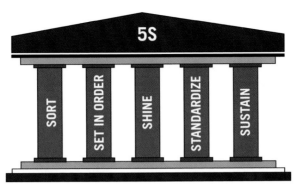

The Second Pillar: Set in Order The second pillar speaks to *orderliness*. Orderliness entails the arrangement of needed materials and equipment so that they are quickly accessible and easy to use. When you achieve orderliness, anyone who comes into your work area will know where equipment, tools, and materials are, and where to put them when they are finished using them. Ordering your resources establishes consistency, which reduces waste, ends aimless searches, and extinguishes excessive motion throughout the workplace. Moving around does not necessarily generate work. Managers must set their work areas in order to maximize the efficiency of workers' efforts.

The Third Pillar: Shine The third pillar emphasizes the removal of dirt, grime, and dust from the work area. Managers must always ensure that the workspace is neat and clean. If your work area and equipment continually remain in top condition, they will be ready for use at any time. Because cleaning occurs on an ongoing basis, the need for tour-ready cleaning is eliminated.

The Fourth Pillar: Standardize The basic purpose of the fourth pillar is to prevent setbacks from the first three pillars. Standardization makes the implementation of sort, set in order, and shine a daily habit and way of life. This ensures that the first three pillars are maintained in their fully implemented state and are consistent across all functional units, including administrative offices. Anyone should be able to distinguish between normal and abnormal conditions at a glance.

The Fifth Pillar: Sustain The fifth pillar dictates discipline: managers must sustain correct procedures over time. No matter how well the first four pillars are implemented, the 5S system will not work for long without a commitment from all managers and their employees to sustain the system. It is the responsibility of everyone to ensure that policies and procedures are adhered to and any violations are addressed immediately.

Centex: 5S at Work!

Centex Machining, a small but successful Round Rock, Texas, company, was an early mover in the niche market of medical contract manufacturing, so competitors were few. Resting on its early laurels, Centex neither sought nor embraced change. Company executives didn't even consider the improvements that could be made by implementing the principles of 5S.

In 2002, Pete Mangan, a former director of operations for Bausch & Lomb, became general manager at Centax. An avid practitioner of the 5S methodology, he quickly began looking for ways to implement the pillars. He discovered that the machining division was effectively operational for only 29 percent of manned hours and revenue-per-employee was just under $78,000 a year. According to Mangan, "Implementing a 5S program was the foundational building block and instrumental in making the changes required to significantly improve these key measures." He developed a team-based strategy to implement his 5S program. This not only generated significant employee engagement—it worked incredibly well.

Being a practitioner of the basics of operations excellence, Mangan knew the importance of measurable improvement. He and his team established seven key operating measures to monitor the effectiveness of the 5S program and hold themselves accountable for results. Focusing on customer requirements, the team identified Lead Time and On-Time Delivery as key customer service measures that needed improvement. The team also determined that addressing cost would bolster both customer satisfaction and the company's profitability. Mangan identified five financial or financially related measures whose improvement could help him manage the business, drive improvement, and increase profitability: Revenue per Employee, Spindle Up Time (the time when machines were actually producing), Scrap, Tooling Costs, and EBITDA (Earnings Before Income, Tax, Depreciation, and Amortization). As you can see in Table 4.1, the results of Mangan's 5S program were nothing short of astounding. Double-digit improvement was recorded for every measure, and six of seven measures improved by more than 35 percent!

Implementation of 5S can spur double-digit improvement in your key operating measures, too!

Table 4.1 Centex's Seven Key Operating Measures

Measure	5S Program Initialization	5S Program Conclusion	Percent Improvement	Impact of Improvement
Lead Time	14 weeks	5 weeks	64%	Centex generated more sales.
On-Time Delivery	86%	95%	10%	The company became more competitive.
Revenue per Employee	$78,000	$132,000	69%	The change impacted EBITDA significantly.
Spindle Up Time	28%	53%	89%	There were increases in capacity, on-time delivery, and employee effectiveness.
Scrap	9%	5%	44%	Costs were reduced.
Tooling Costs	8% of Revenue	5% of Revenue	38%	Profits increased.
EBITDA			10x	The ability to invest increased.

So how exactly did Mangan utilize the five pillars to achieve such stellar results?

→ At the front end of the process, Centex's contract review process was standardized to ensure clarity and understanding of each customer order.

→ Machine centers were divided into cells of five. Each machine center was operated by an experienced machinist, a journeyman, and a trainee.

→ A tool crib was established and maintained. Holding fixtures were inventoried, numbered, and bar coded in standardized storage containers, and tool crib management software was installed. See Figure 4.4 on the next page.

→ Cell cabinets were built for each cell. These cabinets stored a standardized set of color-coded tools and gauges, and the materials required to run each cell.

→ Workers stopped hoarding disposable tools in personal toolboxes.

→ Standard machine sets, vices, and chuck holders were assigned to each machine set-up.

Figure 4.4 Centex's Tool Crib

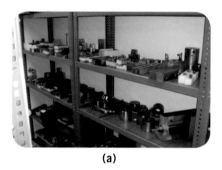 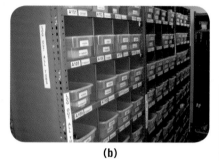

(a)   (b)

Centex's tool crib (a) before Pete Mangan established the five pillars of 5S and (b) after he established the system.

→ A standard tooling set containing 14 common tools was assigned to each machine.

→ Disposable tooling vending machines with automated supplier replenishment processes were implemented within the tool crib management system.

→ A proprietary Golden Standard process was established to manage highly specialized processes without the need for highly specialized employees.

According to Mangan:

> Implementing an integrated 5S program is an absolute requirement for any business today. If you ask any front line operations manager how they spend most of their day they would probably rank "fire fighting" in the top three answers. A 5S program will drastically reduce this and allow you to focus on the future direction of the business.

Although Centex Machining provides a manufacturing example, the principles can easily be applied to any work environment with similar results. If you have not previously been exposed to the pillars of 5S, research the system further. It is an extremely effective team-based approach to creating a safe and clean work environment. It works in manufacturing, back office operations, service operations, and virtually any other work environment. (It works at home, too!) But to be successful, 5S must be practiced by everyone in the organization. From the top-down, every worker must be actively involved in implementation of the pillars. If you can achieve 5S, you can achieve operations excellence!

Teamwork

Teamwork is a critical success factor to the achievement of operations excellence. Your employees work together every day. Some may work in isolation as freelance or contracted contributors, but whether by email or phone, they must still work with others. Leadership teams, chartered teams, project teams, and department-level workgroups must all work as cohesive units to achieve results. Teamwork often crosses departmental and even company boundaries. Because it can involve multiple managers and many individuals, leaders must ensure that all employees understand their importance as well as the processes, policies, and procedures that support them.

That is why effective teamwork is so important to achieving excellence!

A high-performance work environment cannot be achieved without teamwork, but truly outstanding teamwork is a rarity. Teams are made up of people, each of whom has a unique style, opinion, and yes, ego. Getting workers to set aside self-interests and "row together" requires leadership, a goal that everyone can rally around, and an understanding of what is needed for the team to be effective. In the words of Jon M. Huntsman, "There are no one-man teams—either by definition or natural law. Success is a cooperative effort; it's dependent upon those who stand beside you."[5]

POINTERS

Teamwork is achieved when coworkers can come together, put personal agendas aside, understand each others' strengths and weaknesses, and figure out how to work together to win the gold! Picture the United States hockey team that beat Russia and Finland to win the gold medal at the 1980 Winter Olympics or the New York Giants' upset win over the New England Patriots at the 2008 Super Bowl. Even in business, high-performance teams like those at RF Communications, Bausch & Lomb, and FWP can achieve what some believe to be impossible. In *The Five Dysfunctions of a Team*, Patrick Lencioni points out:

If you could get all the people in an organization rowing in the same direction, you could dominate any industry, in any market, against any competition, at any time.[6]

Teams

Effective teams are made up of unique individuals with varying interests, talents, and strengths. As Chapter 3 says, individuals who are placed in challenging roles that align with their talents will be motivated to accomplish more, which helps develop stronger teams. If each team member can recognize the strengths of others, talents will be applied appropriately, and the team will most likely be successful. An effective team is greater than the sum of its parts. Because differing perspectives, knowledge, skills, and talents intersect, teams can develop creative solutions that no single person—not even the most skilled—could have produced alone. This is especially true when teams work across departmental or functional lines, and everyone affected by a problem is represented.

An effective team is comprised of participants serving in four crucial roles:

1. A *team leader* manages the team. She or he calls meetings, assigns action items, oversees administrative details, and acts as a liaison with the sponsor.

2. *Team members* contribute their expertise, ideas, action, and accountability to the team. They should not only participate at meetings but also complete output-related assignments between meetings.

3. A *team facilitator* is a neutral participant who guides members through the quality process, suggests solutions to team problems, and unobtrusively makes sure that all members are allowed to participate fully.

4. A *team sponsor* makes a team's success possible. He or she does not engage in the team's daily activities, but guides the team by securing resources (time, budget, and talent), removing organizational obstacles, and acting as the team's advocate within the organization.

Not all workgroups are teams. Four key criteria must be met for a group to qualify as an effective team:

1. Group members must be willing to work together to develop and implement the outputs required of the team.

2. Group members must be interdependent. A single member

could not achieve the same goals as those achieved by the team in the same way or in the same timeframe. All members of the group must share the workload and depend on the others to contribute some necessary knowledge, skills, or abilities.

3. Members must be selfless. They must be willing to abate their own self-interests so the team can achieve its goals and objectives.

4. The team must have a specific charter, a reason for existing. A charter defines the team's protocol, goals, and methodologies.

The charter is particularly important. It specifies the team's mission, outputs, customers, customer requirements, performance measures, and critical success factors. A charter should also clarify results and boundaries (authority, degree of latitude, resources, limitations, budget, and timeframe). You may notice that these elements mirror those discussed in the context of effective leadership. For a leadership team, the business plan functions as a charter: it defines the company vision, mission, strategy, goals and objectives, initiatives, and means of accountability. Department-, function-, and project-level charters provide similar guidelines, but on wider scales.

For team members, a charter functions like a road map: it tells them where they are, where they're going, and how they're going to get there. It clarifies the team mission and holds all members accountable for delivering results. While often approached hesitantly, the drafting of a team charter does not need to be an administrative nightmare. Charters can be formal or informal, depending on your preference. A one-page charter is adequate for most departmental and project teams, but efforts that are more complex, strategic in nature or long term will require more specificity and detail.

The Basics of Effective Teams

Hundreds of books have been written about team effectiveness. Often their complex theories and principles boil down to just a handful of basic behavioral needs. In *The Five Dysfunctions of a Team*, Patrick Lencioni tackles common dysfunctions that lead to team ineffectiveness. He says that addressing the basic behavioral needs of trust, healthy conflict, commitment, and accountability will steer a team away from dysfunction and toward effectiveness. Here, a new fifth solution to team ineffectiveness—selflessness—is also discussed. Leadership, management, and project teams must understand these five basic behavioral needs if they want to nullify dysfunction, achieve success, and reach a state of excellence.

Trust

As was mentioned earlier, trust is difficult to earn but very easy to lose. Without trust, teams will neither operate effectively nor achieve exceptional results. Trust enables team members to work together, challenge each other, and deliver on expectations. In a trusting team, members:

→ Understand the talents, strengths, and weaknesses that each member brings.

→ Respond to questions, advice, and feedback about assigned tasks and responsibilities without becoming defensive.

→ Are not afraid to ask for help or admit when they've made mistakes.

→ Do not pursue hidden agendas or play politics.

A team without trust operates like a child throwing a tantrum in a toy store. It's not going to go anywhere unless someone pulls it along, kicking and screaming! Anyone with children can sympathize—it's not a pleasant experience.

Healthy Conflict

Have you ever worked in a business environment in which everyone gets along? Have you worked in an office without conflict, confrontation, or challenge? Have you ever been more bored, frustrated, or mistrustful in your entire life? Without trust, teams will never engage in healthy conflict. Without healthy conflict, teams will never arrive at the best solutions. Teams that engage in healthy conflict have interesting meetings and generate the best ideas. They can discuss advantages and disadvantages, develop courses of

When management teams lack trust, they often dance around conflicts that arise, particularly during periods of change. When implementing change involves seemingly endless meetings, team members may lose faith in the process and disengage. For example, some members may disagree with the changes and their implementations and still nod and agree to get the meetings over with as quickly as possible. The empty nod and gestures like it connote a clear deficit in healthy conflict. They also convey a false sense of commitment to team leaders who confuse compliance with enthusiasm. Even if nodding employees leave meetings with the intent of voicing their true opinions to their managers, their nodding behavior in the meetings dissuades conflict, commitment, or both. Passive agreement makes effective teamwork and operational excellence extremely challenging to achieve.

action, and solve problems efficiently. An effective team understands that even if members disagree and 100 percent consensus is never reached, they can still work together to achieve the team's goals.

Commitment

Commitment is a product of the interrelation between a strong charter, universal trust, and healthy conflict. If team members cannot trust each other, they won't engage in healthy discussion or debate. If they can't discuss their ideas, members will never truly commit to the project. For members to develop good ideas, they must clearly understand the direction, purpose, and final goals and objectives of the project, as dictated by the charter. Through trust and healthy conflict, a team can align itself around the objectives of the charter before it actually begins work. If necessary, the team might modify or refine the charter to solidify commitment to the effort.

If the charter, trust, and conflict are all optimized, employees will remain committed to the team and its goals. Even if teamwork falters or goals aren't met as easily as expected, members will recognize and accept mistakes quickly without hesitation and without degradation of commitment. Keeping its goals and objectives in mind, the team will maintain direction, adapt to mistakes and triumphs along the way, and ultimately deliver positive results.

Accountability

Accountability for results is a necessary expectation of every function within an organization. Too often, leaders fail to hold teams accountable for achieving their goals. Some leaders overlook poor performance to maintain harmony. Others do it to avoid offending talented employees that they fear they might lose. It is extremely difficult to repair the damage done to a leader's integrity once managerial cowardice and favoritism become evident. While leaders are responsible for establishing accountability, team members must hold each another accountable as well. This allows them to identify and correct problems quickly: shared accountability ensures that poor performers make improvements or face removal. It also strengthens bonds of respect and teamwork amongst members.

Teams that neglect accountability often exceed budgets, miss project deadlines, and make mistakes that require rework. Some even fail to accomplish basic goals and objectives. Occasionally, team leaders bury abysmal results in copy about business growth so that their superiors can't figure out what the team actually delivered. **Accountability is fundamental to success!** There is no better evidence of accountability's effectiveness than in professional sports. Athletes who do not perform threaten the success of the team. If they can't get it together, they're benched—plain and simple. The constant threat of removal can be a hard reality to accept, but team members must acknowledge responsibility for the tasks assigned to them if they want to be successful and achieve the team's goals.

Selflessness

Selflessness is the single most important behavioral pattern of effective teams. Individual egos, self-interests, and personal agendas must be set aside so that the team can unite and achieve positive results. This is no easy task! When teams are comprised of members who lack selflessness, teamwork disintegrates. If every member pulls the team in a different direction to accomplish individual goals instead of team goals, the team may never reach its destination. If members refuse to accept others' ideas, the best solutions may never be discovered. In short, the damage that selfishness does to a team is often irreparable. High-profile athletes with big egos sometimes come to believe that the game is all about them. If they become a distraction to the team's ultimate objective of winning a championship, this goal will never be reached. If a coach cannot garner the support or authority to bench such arrogant players, his or her effectiveness as a leader diminishes along with that of the team.

On the other hand, if high-profile athletes work together and act selfless-ly, their team's effectiveness will skyrocket. In 1997, the San Antonio Spurs drafted Tim Duncan, who had had an outstanding basketball career at Wake Forest. Duncan joined the team as a power forward, but it was generally un-derstood that he would eventually replace superstar David Robinson as the team's franchise player and center. At 7'1" tall and 250 pounds, Robinson was a formidable presence when he joined the Spurs in 1989. But he was not only large—he was athletically gifted: by the time Duncan joined the Spurs, Robinson had won two college basketball player-of-the-year awards, NBA Rookie of the Year, NBA Defensive Player of the Year, and NBA MVP. Robin-son also held a number of records in scoring, rebounding, and blocked shots. Despite his many accomplishments, Robinson had never led his team to an NBA championship.

While Robinson could have reacted selfishly and refused to accept Dun-can as a teammate when the young rookie was brought in to help the team achieve its goal of an NBA championship, Robinson selflessly mentored his replacement, encouraged his development, and accepted the changing dynamics within the team. In interviews, Robinson was nothing but support-ive of Duncan. As a result of Robinson's selflessness, the San Antonio Spurs won their first NBA championship in 1999. They won their second champi-onship in 2003—the final year of David Robinson's illustrious career.

Whether in sports or business, effective teamwork makes the difference between mediocrity and excellence. Teamwork necessitates trust among members, the ability to have healthy and challenging debates, a strong com-mitment to goals and objectives, accountability for achieving desired results, and selflessness. These five basic behavioral needs are all interdependent and critical to an effective team.

Rewards and Recognition

What comes to mind when you think about rewards and recognition? If your immediate re-sponse is, "We're already paying our employees—now we have to reward them, too?" or "Ugh, another program to make employees happy. Can't we just focus on getting the job done?" then this section will be particularly invaluable to you. It's easy to be critical of rewards and recognition. Some companies establish elaborate reward programs that require hours of administrative effort, cost a lot of money, and appear to deliver little or no value to the organization. Many managers and supervisors find these programs a burdensome waste of time. However, effectively implemented rewards and recognition do not have to be difficult and can deliver immense value.

Every employee likes to know that he or she is doing a good job. Verification that one's output meets or exceeds expectations or that one makes a valuable contribution to the company can be a powerful motivator. But the purpose of effective rewards and recognition is not simply to make your employees feel good—the partnership that is forged between company and employee is just a welcome by-product. By recognizing and rewarding high-quality work, you can set a clear standard of excellence at your operation or company. The acknowledgement of behaviors that are consistent with your values, vision, mission, strategy, and goals increases the likely recurrence of those behaviors. **Engaged employees who have internalized behaviors that reflect a standard of excellence are incalculably valuable to your operation, and your journey toward excellence!**

Rewards are typically embodied by tangible benefits. These include new roles with greater responsibilities, money, trips, tickets to sporting events, opportunities to attend high-level company events, and special certificates. More important to the individual than tangible awards, however, is the acknowledgment that his or her contribution has been noticed and appreciated, and has **made a difference**. Managers have a number of effective options by which to express recognition of an employee:

→ Acknowledge the employee's good work through verbal praise, letters of commendation, or publicly at a monthly or semi-annual meeting.

→ Seek the opinions or input of the employee as a way of showing how much her or his experience is valued.

→ Share information that recognizes the employee as a workplace partner.

→ Champion the employee's participation in strategic company projects because responsibility is a measure of confidence and trust.

→ Take a personal interest in the employee as an individual.

→ Obtain feedback on the employee's performance from customers, and share that feedback in a public forum.

→ Invite the employee to company functions and introduce him or her to senior management. Provide the employee with visibility, and ensure that upper management knows about and values his or her contributions.

→ Recognize the employee in the company or operation newsletter.

→ Simply say "thank you" to the employee!

Rewards and recognition should be formalized to some degree. At FWP, a three-tiered award program provided flexibility for managers who wanted to recognize individual and team achievements. Each of the three awards rewarded employees with tangible, visible recognition for outstanding work:

The **On-The-Spot Award** was given for exemplary initiative, customer service, teamwork, flexibility, community service, or error catching.

The **MVP Award** was given to the employees who best exemplified the company's values.

The **Business Excellence Award** was given to employees who made a significant contribution to business excellence. This prestigious award was subdivided into the categories of customer satisfaction and loyalty, quality and service, innovation, cost reduction, and learning and development.

It is extremely important that rewards and recognition be merited. High ethical standards are paramount in the delivery and management of rewards and recognition programs. When establishing an award, operations leaders must be specific about the necessary requirements for winning and the purpose of the award. Truly effective recognition is bestowed with sincerity, accuracy, and specificity. Rewards and recognition should be granted because they have been earned; favoritism and personal interests should not factor into the selection of the winner. All employees must be eligible for recognition, and all employees should be able to recognize each other's valuable contributions to the workplace. Equalizing rewards and recognition is easier said than done.

Managers must exert a collective effort to maintain consistency!

A rewards and recognition program that is poorly structured or ineffectively managed can have a detrimental effect on employee engagement. It will inhibit other efforts to achieve operational excellence. Because it's such an important decision, operation leaders should take their time when developing a program. Give some thoughtful consideration to the types of rewards and recognition that might work best in your organization. Including employees in the development of a program will increase your chances for success greatly.

Operational Excellence → in Action

People

Process & Technology

Accountability

Leadership

Customers

Life examples of leaders like you.

Ian's Industrial Parts → Fighting It Out!

IMPLEMENTING A NEW OPERATIONAL EFFECTIVENESS STRATEGY at Industrial Parts hasn't been entirely smooth for Ian. Although he has seen improvements in efficiency and increased profit margins, the changes have put pressure on the firm and the workers who were already struggling in the difficult economic environment.

In addition to developing a new strategy, Ian revised his company's operational goals and objectives. To help meet those goals, he formed work teams and reengineered critical production processes to operate more efficiently. The new strategy received positive feedback, but not everyone responded enthusiastically to the new processes. A number of employees were slow to adapt to new ways of doing their work, and some got defensive when supervisors tried to assist them. Everyone was still adjusting to the changes, but struggling employees weren't asking their team leaders for direction to ease the transition.

In the weeks following the reorganization, Ian received several reports from middle managers about workers coming to them with complaints instead of first going to their team leaders. He even received a few worker complaints himself. Other issues weren't brought to the attention of managers or team leaders at all, and quality problems began to surface. Because procedures weren't being followed correctly, the scrap rates on two key components began to creep up. Worst of all, several frustrated workers had even engaged in shouting matches on the production floor over the manufacturing procedures.

Ian is sure that the teams and reengineered processes are ultimately the way to achieve Industrial Parts' strategic goals, but he also realizes that the company won't get very far if he doesn't have an engaged workforce. How can he ease tension among workers and implement his new processes?

Solution:

Ian realizes his workers are struggling with the new team-based approach. Trust, commitment, and accountability have been lacking. Because he received support for the new operational-effectiveness strategy at the outset, he decides to focus on the work teams. By doing so, he hopes to develop a thorough understanding of the new processes, address daily issues, and monitor process performance to meet the company's goals.

Ian pulls his managers together and holds a meeting with each work team. During these sessions, employees give him feedback about what works and what doesn't in the new system. After using the employee feedback to clarify work processes and team roles, he and his managers hold another round of meetings with the teams, at which he explains that each team is responsible for its process and outputs. Team members must work together to identify issues, resolve what they can on their own, and only seek help from management for issues beyond their scope of control. He recommends that teams hold short meetings each morning to discuss successes, identify problems and improvements, and assign owners to each. He gives each team a flip chart that serves as a guide for the team and provides managers with insight into team's daily progress.

By focusing on his people and empowering them to manage their processes, Ian develops an engaged workforce that is able to overcome its resistance to change and work collaboratively to achieve the new goals and objectives.

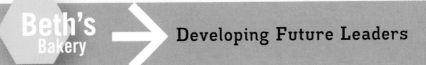

Beth's Bakery ➜ Developing Future Leaders

BETH'S BAKERY HAS GROWN SINCE SHE FIRST BOUGHT IT FROM THE COUNTY (after officials had seized the property from the previous owner after repeated health code violations). The purchase included a fully furnished bakery with industrial baking equipment, appliances, and enough supplies for two storefronts. The original bakery production manager stayed on to work for Beth, as did one storefront manager. As the business grew, Beth added additional store managers, counter clerks, and bakery employees. With her organization quickly approaching 50 employees, Beth wants to explore new ways of expanding her business. However, she wants to make sure that she has people with the right skills to support the growth. How can Beth prepare her organization for the future?

SOLUTION:

Beth concludes that in order to prepare she must do some serious succession planning and put together development plans for her management staff. She begins by defining her current organization structure. She then puts together a plan that defines lead and management positions. She realizes she will need a senior manager who can direct store and operations managers and also step into her shoes as she works to grow the business. She creates individual development plans for her managers by identifying their strengths, weaknesses, and development areas. Beth meets with her management people to communicate the succession planning process, get feedback, and ask for their support. She then meets with each manager individually to plan the development of her staff and the evolution of her leadership team.

Pioneer Processing → Opening Communication Channels

HAVING DEFINED PIONEER PROCESSING SERVICES' VISION, MISSION, STRATEGIES, and supporting goals and objectives, Felix and his leadership team realize that they and their employees have an exciting future. Pioneer Bank's planned growth will have a tremendous impact on PPS. Not only will it affect operations in multiple ways, it will provide opportunity for growth and development for every employee.

With a manageable organization of 300 workers, Felix and his staff have found it relatively easy to keep employees up-to-date on what is going on and how the operation is performing. However, given the size and scope of the scheduled changes, he is concerned that his team will struggle with keeping everyone informed of and involved in the planned growth. What should Felix do to ensure that every PPS employee understands the changes being made to operations?

SOLUTION:

Felix and his team realize that one of the keys to keeping employees involved is communication. Their current approach to communication, which utilizes bulletin boards, email, manager communications, and an annual company meeting, simply won't be sufficient.

First, his team agrees to implement an internal website for communicating PPS's vision, mission, strategy, and goals to employees. They solicit employee volunteers to develop the website and post updates regarding planned changes, upcoming events, process improvements, and job opportunities. Felix and his team challenge the website development group to be creative and develop a website that employees will use and of which they can be proud.

To ensure that senior management is visible and engaged with employees, Felix and his team agree to hold semiannual all-employee meetings where they will update employees on the progress they are making toward their annual goals and inform them of how the business is developing as a whole.

Finally, Felix decides to publish a quarterly newsletter to disseminate important information about PPS, such as customer feedback and business performance. The newsletter will also include a question-and-answer section so that employees can get answers to virtually any question they have about the business.

THE ANNUAL REPORT SNUCK UP ON TREVOR THIS YEAR. Every year since he started Tech Reports, he and Teresa have posted a special end-of-year report to the Tech Reports blog. The report recaps the big news stories of the year and profiles the top ten companies that Trevor and Teresa think have the greatest potential to introduce a game-changing new product in the coming year. The Annual Tech Report gets a lot of attention from the blog's regular readers and offers many new readers an introduction to the other services provided by Tech Reports.

Trevor has done some outlining, and after processing an intense brainstorming session with Teresa, he has identified trends and companies that he wants to highlight. However, he hasn't yet finished the hard research or spoken with his industry contacts. While he wants to double the size of the report by offering a broad look into the direction of the industry and highlighting major players in each sub-industry, Trevor isn't sure that he can manage the scope of the project while still addressing several critical news stories that he's been covering and the day-to-day responsibilities of managing his growing operation. How can Trevor finish a top-notch product without sacrificing his other work?

SOLUTION:

Trevor decided to build a team to do the bulk of the research and writing of the report. The team has four basic roles that need to be filled. Because he needed to free up time to manage his other work, Trevor took on the role of team sponsor. He promised to resist the urge to micromanage, but offered to provide resources such as internal and external contacts. Teresa volunteered to be the team leader since she had worked on the annual report before and had helped with the brainstorming. With Teresa at the helm, Trevor could be confident in the quality of the report.

Trevor chose three research assistants as team members. Tabatha is good at reading through filings and reports, analyzing numbers, and distilling data in an organized and easily understandable manner. Tommy is one of Trevor's best interviewers. And Tommy is good at unearthing obscure sources and digging beyond the major headlines. Finally, Trevor chose Takashi as his team facilitator because while he encourages writers to have strong opinions, Takashi can manage any arguments that arise as the project moves forward.

THE BUZZ

→ Leaders are responsible for establishing a vision and creating an environment that breeds high performance, but it is through the talent and the power of your organization's people that operational excellence becomes a reality.

→ Values are the foundation of the operations excellence model, the base upon which your behaviors rest. Establishing a foundation built on the values of trust, respect, and integrity enables leaders to create a high-performance work environment.

→ Engagement results in consistent and constructive action on behalf of the customer by every employee. Engagement is not an action, nor is it something that you can give to people. Employee engagement is a result!

→ A high-performance work environment is one in which individual strengths are put to use where they can best serve the company and its employees. It's an environment in which employees get to do what they do best every day, in which there is organizational clarity, and in which employees work together toward common goals and objectives.

→ There are five practical steps for achieving management effectiveness in the real world: select great people, define roles and responsibilities, establish accountability, educate and develop, and show that you care.

→ The five pillars of a safe and efficient operation are: sort, set in order, shine, standardize, and sustain. If operations professionals follow these five directives, they will establish a safer, more excellent work environment.

→ A high-performance work environment cannot be achieved without teamwork. Effective teams are made up of unique individuals with varying interests, talents, and strengths. Trust, healthy conflict, commitment, accountability, and selflessness will steer a team away from dysfunction and toward effectiveness.

→ By recognizing and rewarding high-quality work, you can set a clear standard of excellence at your operation or company. The acknowledgement of behaviors that are consistent with your values, vision, mission, strategy, and goals increases the likely recurrence of those behaviors.

Notes: [1] Smart, Bradford D. *Topgrading*. Paramus: Prentice Hall Press, 1999; [2] Buckingham, Marcus, and Curt Coffman. *First, Break All the Rules*. New York: Simon & Schuster, 1999; [3] Buckingham, Marcus. *The One Thing You Need to Know*. New York: Free Press, 2005; [4] Ibid; [5] Huntsman, Jon M. *Winners Never Cheat*. Paramus: Prentice Hall Press, 2005; [6] Lencioni, Patrick. *The Five Dysfunctions of a Team*. San Francisco: Jossey-Bass, Inc., 2002.

Process and
Technology

5

U nless you're an operations professional, the importance of processes and process management may not be entirely clear. Simply stated, a process is a set of activities that when performed together provide value for an internal or external customer. Processes are the means by which we get things done. When we assemble products, deliver services, and manage operations, we do so using processes. The quality of your products and services is determined not only by their design but also by the quality of the processes used to create, produce, and deliver them. Because they are so important, processes should be precisely defined, accurately documented, and effectively managed to meet or exceed the dynamic needs of customers. Operations excellence cannot be achieved without effective processes or process management.

Technology is an enabler of processes. When applied correctly, technology increases customer and operational value by improving the effectiveness and efficiency of your processes. Too often the development of a new technology is approached as a business strategy in and of itself. Some leaders spend more time and energy on discovering and implementing the next great technology than on understanding its impact on established processes. **Great operations professionals know that they should never pursue a technology without first considering the processes that it will impact.** A failure to realize that process and technology are intrinsically linked can lead to disastrous results.

For processes to be effective, they and their enabling technologies must be understood end-to-end, integrated tightly, appropriately implemented, and managed in a disciplined way!

Process Management

Processes can be grouped into three logical types: management processes, core processes, and support processes. Each must be effective in order to have operations excellence.

Management processes guide and govern your core processes, ensuring that there is predictability in their output and performance. Some examples include strategic business planning, business policies and procedures, business performance management, and quality management.

Core processes create customer value and are often specific to particular business units. Some examples include product development, operational capability and service development, manufacturing or production, and transaction processing, such as new account and claims processing. Core processes typically link directly to your external customers' requirements.

Support processes enable your management and core processes to achieve their desired intent. Examples include human resources recruiting and succession planning, procurement processes, and risk and compliance processes.

For any of these processes to be effective, they must be managed with discipline. Disciplined business process management is achieved through five fundamental practices:

1. **Process definition**
2. **Standard Operating Procedures**
3. **Process change management**
4. **Process measurement**
5. **Quality Assurance and Quality Control**

You may already be familiar with some or all of these five practices. Each is important to effective process management, and therefore must be championed by every operations leader.

Process Definition

The processes that are core to your business and critical to meeting all of your customer and business requirements must be defined: **the who, what, where, when, why, and how of each and every process must be clearly documented.** *Process definitions* should be meticulously maintained and updated when necessary. They should be deeply engrained in the minds of the employees and managers who are responsible for them. This may sound simple enough, but more business and operations leaders than you might imagine overlook it.

Failure to define processes is a fundamental weakness. Employees may know how to execute specific tasks, but because there is no established baseline from which to work, they cannot understand the purpose or impact of their actions within the end-to-end process. This breeds inefficiency, diminishes quality, and incurs business risk—three factors that inhibit operations excellence.

Surprisingly, many companies choose not to define their processes. This is true for both small and large companies—including some well-known industry leaders. Instead, they rely on the *institutional knowledge* of their employees to ensure that processes operate as they should. Unfortunately, institutional knowledge can only take a company so far. Without documentation, it becomes extremely difficult to train new employees, transition to new sites, solve complex problems, and approach sustainable process improvement. Expensive specialists and external consultants are typically hired to accomplish these tasks. Eventually, this *institutional knowledge syndrome* will cause even basic processes to deteriorate; managing employees, responding to customer satisfaction issues, handling day-to-day operations, and maintaining overall business performance becomes burdensome.

If institutional knowledge syndrome is a disease, then process definition is its cure. Your approach to definition and documentation should be straightforward, logical, and cost effective. See Figure 5.1. The last thing you want is an administrative nightmare. All three types of processes (management, core, and support) should be defined. For each type, your most important processes are those that are critical to meeting your customers' requirements, so these are the first processes to define. A number of tools and software applications are available to help you document your processes,

Figure 5.1 Two Distinct Methods of Process Documentation

Document Processing Process

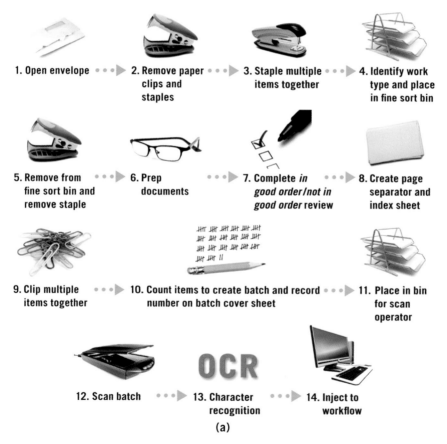

1. Open envelope
2. Remove paper clips and staples
3. Staple multiple items together
4. Identify work type and place in fine sort bin
5. Remove from fine sort bin and remove staple
6. Prep documents
7. Complete *in good order/not in good order* review
8. Create page separator and index sheet
9. Clip multiple items together
10. Count items to create batch and record number on batch cover sheet
11. Place in bin for scan operator
12. Scan batch
13. Character recognition
14. Inject to workflow

(a)

This figure exemplifies two distinct methods of process documentation: (a) setting illustrative depictions alongside directive text, and (b) using a standard flow charting system. Depending on how critical the process and the need for further clarity, each step in the process may require from the very basic—such as Microsoft's PowerPoint and Visio—to the advanced—such as iGrafx's Process, Metastorm's ProVision, and IBM's Websphere Business Modeler. Whatever path you take, **keep it simple!** Defining and documenting key processes is also tremendously beneficial to the development of standard operating procedures, a topic that will be addressed in the following section. As you document your methods, you might find yourself challenging established practices. In doing so, you will minimize waste, optimize efficiency, and pave the way for future improvements.

Product and Service Development

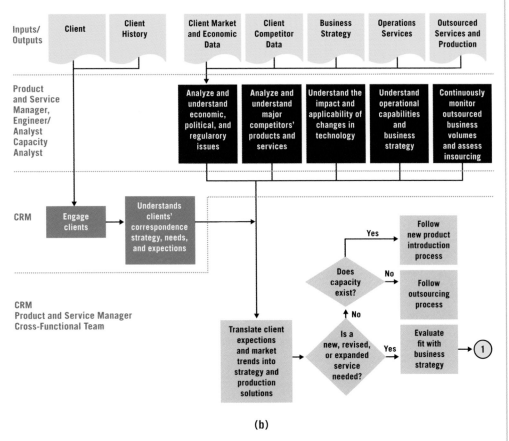

(b)

additional detail. Ensure that your processes are documented in a way that is easily understood and can be archived and maintained so that process definitions remain current relative to changing customer needs and business improvement efforts.

Standard Operating Procedures

Have you ever purchased a new, unassembled bicycle or piece of furniture? Did you pull the parts from the box and without referencing the instructions attempt to assemble the thing? Were you surprised when there were more than a few parts left over? You might have wondered to yourself, "What did I overlook?" It's simple: you did not follow the provided procedures. In the world of business, disregarding procedure has similar consequences. When procedural mistakes are made, they can cost a company money, damage its reputation, and in some cases, threaten the very existence of the organization.

> To prevent procedural error and stay on the road to operations excellence, you must implement process management practices.

Standard Operating Procedures (SOPs) are the standardized means by which processes operate. Essentially, they define the "how" by dictating optimized operation. Procedures improve operation success by institutionalizing information that had previously been entrusted to employees' memories. When a procedure is written, personal knowledge becomes common knowledge. SOPs are important for several reasons:

1. They provide means of reference for both new and senior employees.
2. They dictate consistent methods for performing processes.
3. They improve efficiency and decrease variation.
4. They facilitate error correction and problem solving when something goes wrong.
5. They ensure the safety and well-being of your employees.
6. They provide documented methods for implementing change and ensuring process consistency.
7. They support mobility of processes from one site to another.
8. They combat institutional knowledge syndrome.

After you establish SOPs, you should strive to follow them consistently and correctly. When they become operationally normative, SOPs serve as standard baselines for measuring progress along the road to excellence.

Modifications to processes and related procedures will affect your SOPs. If you're sensitive to the positive and negative effects that changes have on your SOPs, charting a new course for your business will become less like guesswork. Meeting the changing needs and expectations of your customers should not disrupt your established and functioning SOPs.

When developing and documenting your SOPs, be sure to **keep it simple!** Too often, business leaders do too much too quickly, which leads to an abundance of administrative headaches. Instead, managers should key in on their critical processes. They should document their most important and often-used procedures in a simple, concise, and manageable format. The proliferation of digital record keeping and online training has led to the popularization of a variety of document creation and database software options. These tools have made defining processes, creating SOPs, and maintaining process definitions easier and more efficient than ever. Microsoft Word may suit the needs of smaller, budget-conscious businesses, while enterprise content management applications such as EMC's Documentum and Xerox's DocuShare may be more suitable for larger organizations. Depending on your needs, you may also want to invest in software that schedules employee training, tracks development, or catalogs artifacts and information related to your products, services, and processes.

Remember that once your processes and procedures are documented, they will be used as learning tools. They will be referenced when changes are made to processes and when re-education becomes necessary. The easier your SOPs are to understand, access, and manage, the more effective and efficient your employees will be.

Process Change Management

When engineers make changes to existing products, they must document both the original design and every change that they make. Changes to electronic circuitry, printed circuit board layouts, design plans, and schedules must all be recorded. If an engineer fails to document the original design, he or she may lose track of the starting point. If the engineer fails to document changes, he or she may not remember what was modified, what worked, and what didn't. In the absence of adequate change management, engineers simply cannot work effectively.

The same is true for you and your business. To meet shifting customer demands, your products and services will inevitably require change. So too will the processes and procedures that produce them. If you do not document these changes, you will lose track of progress, experience redundancy, and possibly reintroduce items that were removed for a good reason. (Further, failure to document processes could put you on the wrong side of the Sarbanes-Oxley Act of 2002.) To maintain consistency in operational performance and quality throughout a change, **it is critically important that you establish an effective *process change management system.***

Immediately after you define and document a process, you should create and begin to maintain a record of all changes made to that process. Notes on the changes' purpose, performance, and execution should accompany basic details so employees can readily understand every aspect of the change when they reference the change record. A disciplined approach to process change management ensures that your processes perform consistently, meet all regulatory requirements, satisfy your risk management policies, and meet your customer requirements—regardless of the changes you make.

Process Measurement

Are your processes capable of meeting your customer requirements? Do you get consistent results day after day? Do you know exactly how well your processes are performing? If you don't know the answers to these questions, then *process measurement*—the fourth fundamental practice of effective process management—is not present in your operation. Process measurement allows you to understand the full capabilities of your processes. By collecting the data necessary to monitor and improve your processes over time, you can ensure that desired outputs are achieved, quality standards are met, waste is minimized, and resources are utilized in an efficient, effective, and safe manner. Process measurement allows you to deliver consistently on both internal and external customer expectations.

In addition to broadening your knowledge of existing processes, process measurement provides a baseline from which improvements can be made. If you want to reduce the time it takes to produce quarterly financial statements, set up a new customer account, or manufacture a car, simple process measurements can guide your improvement and investment decisions and provide accountability for results. The importance of measurement will be addressed at length in Chapter 6.

Quality Assurance and Quality Control: Building Quality into Your Processes

Have you ever worked for an operation where goods or services always seemed to need rework? Did the product design team not engage with operations to develop an effective way to produce or deliver the product to the end customer? Did an endless number of changes and redirections frustrate you, your staff, and your customers? Did a new product simply not fit with your operational capabilities, making it extremely difficult to produce or service? When operations fail to work collaboratively with all parts of the business or ensure that quality is built into the design, development, and delivery of their products, customers and employees quickly become unhappy, unmotivated, and disengaged. You might expect that such operations are things of the past. Unfortunately, even in today's competitive environment, they are still quite common. Quality should be an absolute given, an unspoken word. If you have to talk about or focus specifically on quality, you are already in a losing position. Quality should be an indivisible part of your culture. It should be felt immediately in the ways you conduct business, develop products, and provide your services every day.

Quality Assurance and Quality Control are key elements of a Quality Management System, which is rooted in the basics of operations excellence. Although a detailed discussion of Quality Management Systems is beyond the scope of this text, Quality Assurance and Quality Control are fundamental to effective business process management and to the achievement of operations excellence.

Quality Assurance is an all-encompassing system of processes that bolster quality and empower quality management. Quality Assurance provides the manager of a business's processes with a mandate to ensure that quality is built into everything the operation does. In other words, the primary objective of Quality Assurance is to guarantee that internal and external customer requirements are met or exceeded at every level of operations. The most efficient and effective method of guaranteeing quality is through *prevention*. If employees do things right the first time, they will not have to apply the duct tape later. You must build quality into your processes, products, and services from the beginning.

Quality through prevention precludes quality through inspection—or worse—quality through accident.

Some examples of Quality Assurance processes are:

1. Internal and external customer surveys

2. Product design and delivery reviews by product development and operations management teams

3. Design for manufacturability reviews by design engineering and operations management teams

4. New product introductions and walkthroughs

5. Supplier certification programs

Quality Control is a system of processes used to monitor variation in processes, products, and services. Quality Control ensures that an acceptable level of consistency is maintained in process outputs and that products and services conform to established standards. Quality Control necessitates careful monitoring, data collection, and analysis of process inputs, the process itself, and process outputs. Some examples of Quality Control processes are:

1. Checkpoints and work sampling at key control points to maintain consistency in process output

2. Process audits to ensure that processes are executed as designed and documented

3. Facility safety audits to ensure compliance with safety standards

4. Housekeeping audits to maintain order and cleanliness

5. Supplier inspections to monitor process controls and ensure that products and services meet specifications

6. Root cause analysis and corrective action processes to resolve service issues, defects, and deficiencies

Quality Assurance and Quality Control are both critically important to effective process management and the achievement of operations excellence, but they only work if quality is a way of life within the operation. Too often, the employees who carry out Quality Assurance and Quality Control functions are looked upon as obstructionists by those who produce and deliver the product or provide customer service. This perception is a barrier to operations excellence. Whether directly or indirectly, each employee contributes to the quality of a business's products or services. Quality Assurance and Quality Control professionals provide oversight, guidance, and support, ensuring that employees can meet customer requirements consistently. To make sure that a high level of quality is maintained, it is incumbent upon leadership to create an organizational culture that lives and breathes quality. This maximizes the effectiveness of Quality Assurance and Quality Control, which drives customer satisfaction and loyalty, which in turn helps sustain long-term business growth and profitability.

Companies often focus and refocus on quality as they navigate business cycles. As such, quality and topics related to quality have been popular subjects for decades. Many fantastic books have been written about quality, Quality Assurance, and Quality Control. The following four books are great resources toward the development of a well-rounded understanding of quality and how to drive process excellence:

1. Joseph M. Juran and Joseph A. De Feo, *Juran's Quality Handbook*

2. Philip B. Crosby, *Quality Is Free*

3. Kaoru Ishikawa, *Guide to Quality Control*

4. Mary Walton, *The Deming Management Method*

Membership in the American Society for Quality (ASQ) is also highly recommended. It allows you to stay abreast of news, events, and conferences related to quality. It also provides you with a dedicated network of professional contacts with whom to share information, methodologies, and ideas on quality management.

Technology and Innovation

Customers' needs and expectations change almost daily. Operations leaders who are passionate about excellence know that simply upgrading established processes won't improve business or expand customer reach; they search constantly for new and better ways to exceed customer expectations. They frequently ask themselves, "What should we do?" and "What's the best way to do it?" These leaders know that to stay ahead of the competition, they must develop new products and services and expand their operational capabilities to deliver them. This type of innovation takes both creative thought and ingenuity.

Innovative value-add technologies improve operational effectiveness and provide tremendous customer value!

If you have a metrics-based performance management process, maintain active listening posts, and have your thumb on the pulse of the industry, then you have the data and business intelligence necessary to guide your technological decision making. Still, to spur creative thought, avoid common pitfalls, and ensure that the decisions you make are the right ones, you'll need additional knowledge about technology investment and benchmarking.

Five Facts about Technology

If you try to talk to any business or operations executive about technology, he or she is likely to cringe. Why is technology such a distasteful subject? Many executives find it frustrating because (1) it is expensive, and (2) the asserted value of technologic investments is often difficult to realize. Understanding and accepting the following basic facts about technology will minimize the frustration and anxiety that typically envelop technology investment decisions. If you keep these facts in mind and stick to a disciplined evaluation, acquisition, and implementation process, the success rates of your technology implementations will increase tenfold.

Fact One: Your technology group loves technology! Technology is their passion. That's why they're in the field. Because they're eager to implement new technologies, not all technology leaders consider the total impact that their investment decisions have on the business. Therefore, there are certain decisions your IT people should not make, and many more that they should not make in a vacuum. Jeanne W. Ross and Peter Weill suggest in their excellent article "Six IT Decisions Your IT People Shouldn't Make" (*Harvard Business Review,* November 2002) that in top-performing companies, senior managers must take leadership roles in key IT decisions. When senior managers abdicate responsibility for these decisions to singular individuals, disaster usually follows. Manager-led decisions should include:

→ How much money should we spend on IT and technology in general?

→ Which business processes should receive technology investment funding?

→ Which IT capabilities need to be distributed company-wide?

→ How good do our IT services really need to be?

→ What security and privacy risks will we accept?

→ Whom do we hold accountable if an IT or technology initiative fails?

These decisions are best made by a strategic leadership team that can bring some balance to the idealism of your chief information or technology officer. Because the answers to these questions must align with your business's overarching vision, mission, and strategies, they should be decided by an impartial and knowledgeable leadership team. IT projects that require a significant investment, carry an extended implementation time, and are critical to your organization's mission should be overseen by executive-level leadership steering committees to ensure periodic reviews of the initiative's progress, issues, and challenges. This process enables leadership to act swiftly in the event that progress is slow, commitments are not being met, or budgets begin to overrun the originally planned investment.

Fact Two: Software and equipment vendors are in the business of selling software and equipment! Vendors want to help you solve your business problems, but their primary objectives are to beat their competition, grow their businesses, and get their products into your operation. Never forget that vendors' foremost concern is revenue. In the interest of meeting their goals and objectives, vendors sometimes push *vaporware*—software and technology that lacks real, tested, and effective functionality. Even if it isn't vaporware, an out-of-the-box technology solution will very rarely meet all of a business's needs. Therefore, it can be challenging to predict the full financial impact of the development and implementation necessary to solve a business's specific problems. The result: costly customization!

Software and equipment demonstrations are intended to wow you, grab your interest, and make you think of all the improvements that the product could deliver to your business. The demo is a lot like a new car pitch—the salesman's goal is to get you into the car! Once you see all the features, feel the ride, and experience that new car feeling, you're hooked! If you decide that a new technology is truly worth your investment after considering and reviewing a pitch, be sure not to rush things. When moving forward with new technology investments, **the devil is in the details!** Accountability for making smart technology and equipment decisions is yours: examine the technology thoroughly, conduct competitive analyses, utilize a trial period

When Daryl Hunt, senior vice president of operations, led a major investment in new mail insertion equipment at FWP, his management team conducted a detailed analysis of two competing high-end equipment providers before investing in the new machines. It performed a run-off test on the production floor to evaluate the set-up times, functionalities, ergonomics, and performances of the competing providers' equipment options. Ultimately though, the final decision of which machines to purchase was made by the operators on the floor. Because they would be using the equipment day-in and day-out, their opinions were of utmost importance. Their final decision yielded an equipment choice that increased capacity, used fewer machines, boosted productivity by over 50 percent, cut maintenance costs, improved overall quality, and expedited customer delivery. By carefully weighing options and methodically testing functionality, a successful solution was achieved!

(if available), read contracts, review warranties, and always establish detailed deliverables and performance expectations. If vendors truly believe in their products, they will commit to your expectations in writing.

Fact Three: Technology investments must align with and support your business strategies. Never invest in technology for technology's sake—unless you have money to burn—because that's exactly what you'll do. Technology should always accomplish two goals: (1) enable and strengthen your business strategies, and (2) provide value to your customers.

If you cannot quantify the value that your investment will deliver or justify the technology's worth to customers, then the probability that the technology will deliver on your expectations is probably pretty close to zero. There are exceptions to this rule, however. A handful of technology initiatives cannot be justified on their own merit, but are still worth pursuing. This is sometimes referred to as "investing in keeping the lights on." Investments to expand server capacities, increase the response time of applications, and upgrade system hardware are important in maintaining the productivity and capabilities of your business and its employees. These infrastructure investments require strategic investment planning by the leadership team so that they can be funded and managed effectively.

Fact Four: Large information management and production execution systems cannot generate measurable value or justifiable ROI on their own merits. The real value of systems such as Enterprise Resource Planning (ERP), Material Requirements Planning (MRP), and Customer Relationship Management (CRM) lies in the new and redesigned business processes that are implemented in advance of or in conjunction with these types of systems. Process should always come before technology. Too many organizations are unwilling to examine existing processes before making a significant financial commitment to technology. They ultimately pay a price for this misstep. Statistics derived by trade periodical *Industrial Management* indicate that "between 50 percent and 75 percent of U.S. firms experience some degree of failure when implementing advance manufacturing or information technology" solutions.[1] According to *Industrial Management*, the top five causes of implementation failure are:

1. Poor leadership by top management
2. Existing business processes that require total reengineering
3. Unrealistic expectations
4. Poor project management
5. Inadequate education and training

Education and training are especially important to the change management activities that support major technology and equipment implementations. Change management is often the first function targeted for cuts when large technology implementations go over budget, which they often do.

Fact Five: Technology initiatives must adhere to the same five critical success factors as all other initiatives. The five critical success factors that apply to operations initiatives (introduced in Chapter 3) also apply to technology initiatives. First, all technology initiatives must be tied to a business strategy. If your technology initiatives don't support a strategy or help move you toward your vision, you should ask yourself, "why are we doing this?"

Second, technology initiatives should have an executive sponsor and a single owner who is accountable for success. An executive sponsor validates the investment and ensures that the initiative has the proper support, guidance, funding, and resources to be successful. A single owner provides

In 1998, Fidelity Wide Processing implemented an Enterprise Resource Planning system, and FWP management was tasked with reengineering the operation's manufacturing and business processes in parallel with the ERP implementation. In short, management had to improve FWP's bottom line and generate the funding for the ERP implementation. By exploring a variety of strategies, the company's top managers identified $14 to $30 million in potential savings, and were ultimately able to generate $20 million worth of improvements to fund the new technology. In turn, the ERP system provided FWP with data and information that enabled management to make better business decisions and manage the operation more effectively.

clarity of responsibility and eliminates finger pointing. **You'll always know who to hold accountable!**

Third, technology initiatives must drive at least one of the business's key operating measures in a positive direction. This provides tangible evidence of value creation.

Fourth, technology initiatives must have clear, quantifiable goals and objectives that are tied to metrics you can use to measure success. What specifically will be achieved through the initiative's implementation? Will you realize an increase in revenue, capacity, or system uptime? Will productivity, quality, or customer service improve? Will the initiative help drive down cost?

Finally, all technology initiatives should have a documented business case and post-completion audit to ensure that the owner delivered on expectations, budgets were adhered to, goals and objectives were met, and measurable positive results were achieved.

Operational
Excellence
in Action

Process &
Technology

Accountability

Life examples of leaders
like you.

Customers

People

Leadership

Ian's
Industrial Parts → A New Production Line

A NUMBER OF YEARS AGO, AN INSATIABLE DEMAND FOR LARGE TRUCKS, SUVs, and massive industrial equipment with large, powerful engines drove Ian's revenue through the roof. Today, the needs of consumers and industrial purchasers alike are changing. Buyers want smaller, fuel-efficient cars and machines that employ arrays of smaller electric power sources. As a result of the shift in demand, many of the company's high-volume parts are no longer selling well.

Ian knows that he has to shift his production to keep up with changing customer needs. After examining a sampling of the parts desired by the customers that support the new product lines, he concludes that his operation faces major changes ahead. Many of the new parts require fewer processing steps and fewer components to assemble. Tooling and fixtures will have to be replaced, and assembly lines and workflows will have to be shrunk and cellularized to be more effective. He knows that while some of these process adjustments will be arduous, they will ultimately free up space, allowing the business to expand capacity and grow in its current facility. Moreover, demand for the earlier model parts has not dried up entirely, so Ian will have to adapt without switching his production focus entirely. What steps does he need to take to make the necessary changes to his production process?

Solution:

Ian knows documentation is the key to successful process change management. He also knows that as workers assemble the new parts, they will find new ways to improve the process and the quality of the parts they produce. For these reasons, his engineers document the details of the new production process and follow the company's change management process religiously. They record each change as well as the impact it has on quality, efficiency, and overall cost. They ensure that the new manufacturing process is carefully laid out and every step of production is described clearly and explicitly. Because Ian knows worker input is critical to creating an efficient and effective process, he instructs the production employees responsible for manufacturing the new parts to engage in the process design.

Once the new process is properly documented, the production team runs a short test to validate the process and identify control points at which quality controls or checks should be implemented to maintain consistency in output. The team also identifies the critical metrics that must be monitored in order to ensure that quality, delivery, and cost goals are met.

With the new process documented and validated, the production team conducts its first pilot production run. From here, team members establish a performance baseline from which they can document changes to the process and record corresponding impacts on their metrics. Finally, they gather additional information about the performance of the parts they produce through customer listening posts, allowing them to make additional process adjustments as needed to meet customer expectations consistently.

Buying a New Oven

AFTER YEARS OF HARD USE, THE ANCIENT OVENS Beth acquired when she bought the bakery are finally coming to the end of their useful lives. Given the estimated cost of maintaining the old ovens, she determines she can probably buy four new ones at a reasonable cost. She theorizes that new equipment might even be more efficient and less costly to operate.

With the goal of improving her morning baking process, Beth starts shopping around for new ovens. After searching the web and visiting two local restaurant equipment suppliers, she discovers there are many options when it comes to industrial ovens. Simple workman ovens sit next to ovens with LCD screens, dual-temperature zones, and voice-recognition capabilities. She is amazed by the advanced technology and wide array of functions, but the high prices of some of the top-of-the-line models give her pause. Furthermore, she is overwhelmed by the vendors' grand promises of astonishing process improvement through more precise temperature settings and computer-controlled timers. With all the choices available, how can Beth make a smart decision for her business?

SOLUTION:

Beth realizes that the oven vendors are knowledgeable about their products and proud of the capabilities they provide, but she also knows they do not fully understand her baking operation or her specific business needs. She starts her decision-making process by looking at her budget, long-term strategic goals, and production needs.

Based on her current budget, Beth is able to eliminate several top models. While many of these models provide increased functionality and options, from a production standpoint baking bread is not a complicated process. She determines she doesn't need bells and whistles; she needs a reliable, well-built oven that can maintain a steady temperature. However, she is willing to pay a little extra for an oven with a greater shelf capacity because that would allow her to produce larger quantities during each baking cycle.

When considering her long-term strategy, Beth decides that managing costs is paramount. This is the one factor that might make it worthwhile to look at technologically advanced models. While an energy-efficient model might cost more up front, keeping costs down in the long run would most certainly pay off.

By examining each oven's total cost of ownership, Beth calculates the return she can expect on her investment. Basing her decision on value, she makes the choice that best fulfills her needs. By effectively monitoring each oven's performance, she can validate that the new ovens deliver on her expectations.

 **Finding a Better Way!**

COMPETITION IN THE PROCESSING INDUSTRY IS FIERCE—especially during a global recession. As Felix and his leadership team begin to develop processes to support the company's new direction, they realize that larger volumes are going to result in considerable increases in headcount. In order to stay competitive and provide more value to their internal customers, they decide to look for ways to eliminate much of the manual work.

Although PPS has effectively implemented form design standards supporting document imaging, its recognition technology can only determine whether or not text is present. If PPS acquires a technology that recognizes individual characters, employees would be able to use the technology to pre-fill forms for current external customers, and new customers would be able to fill out and submit forms online. The technology could also drastically reduce the workloads of employees downstream in the process, providing more time to build customer relationships and grow the business.

Felix's chief information officer says there are a number of suppliers in the marketplace that provide character recognition technology, but because it will be a significant investment and drive major changes to the processes, he and his team will have to make sure that they make a smart choice. How should he approach what could be a major innovation for Pioneer Financial?

Solution:

Felix decides to pull together a cross-functional team with operations and IT leaders from Pioneer Processing and his current internal customers. He tells the team that its objective is to conduct a feasibility study to determine whether advanced recognition technology (1) actually works and (2) is capable of delivering significant value to the business and its end customers. The team develops a straightforward plan to arrive at a comprehensive and conclusive recommendation.

First, team members conduct industry research to determine which of the companies that specialize in recognition technology are considered leaders in the field. Based on specific criteria derived from this research, they determine the top five suppliers with whom they should engage.

Second, they schedule product reviews and demonstrations with each of the five suppliers. Based on these reviews and benchmark data from the suppliers' top customers, they reject those suppliers that do not have fully developed capabilities.

Third, team members establish key measures and use these to determine whether the technology will provide value. Measures like percent of characters recognized, document throughput time, recognition accuracy, and percent of documents processed without human intervention are developed.

Fourth, the team conducts a test (a production pilot) with each remaining vendor to determine each technology's ease of use and effectiveness. During these tests, team members collect input and feedback from employees who process work every day and evaluate the sound performance data provided by the key measures.

Finally, team members compare test results to their current processing environment, determining the value potential of each vendor's character recognition technology from the perspectives of quality, service, cost, and ease of use. With all of this information, the team confidently makes a final recommendation as to whether PPS should pursue this innovation investment and, if it should, with which vendor.

EVER SINCE THE ORANGE COMPUTER NEWS LEAK, Trevor has felt generally uneasy about his sources. While as journalists he and Teresa both know how important it is to make sure that every source is airtight, Trevor is also very aware of the kinds of mistakes that can happen when time constraints occur and unclear instructions are given. As was the case with the Orange report, sensitive news might be delivered across the wrong medium or information might not be quite correct. When these things happen, customers become dissatisfied with Trevor's service, his reputation is tarnished, and the success of the business is jeopardized.

Fearful that he might lose more clients as a result of an error, Trevor has shied away from sensational blog posts and intrepid consultation. Several clients have complained that he's lost his pizzazz, suggesting that his advice has been overly tepid recently. Trevor knows that something has to change. What can he do to ensure that assignments are communicated properly, reports are delivered to the right medium (and in the right format), and that information is properly sourced, accurate, and verified?

SOLUTION:

In order to regain his verve, Trevor must be confident in his company's ability to research, write, and deliver quality reports. Instilling quality assurance in these processes will help ensure that mistakes are prevented and an incident like the Orange Computer news leak never happens again.

Trevor decides that above all else, he must build quality into his processes for assigning and delivering reports. To do this, he creates a simple worksheet to manage both the quality of his processes and his employees' output. When an assignment is delivered to be posted, he requires that the report author also submit the worksheet, which calls for critical information such as what the assignment is about, when and to what medium the report should be posted, a list of sources used in creating the report, and specific instructions as to how sensitive information should be handled.

Although the worksheet takes time to prepare and writers were initially unhappy with the new requirement, Trevor's approach helps ensure that expectations and requirements are clearly communicated to the writers and that those expectations are met and double-checked and that posting instructions are properly documented. Trevor's is a simple solution to a problem that could have had a disastrous effect on his business. Filed worksheets ensure accountability and provide guidance to employees who may need additional training or education should a problem arise. Simply by deciding to build quality into his process, Trevor feels safe to return to the style of reporting that made him successful.

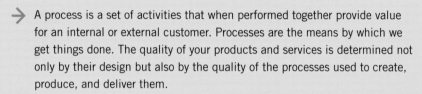

THE BUZZ

→ A process is a set of activities that when performed together provide value for an internal or external customer. Processes are the means by which we get things done. The quality of your products and services is determined not only by their design but also by the quality of the processes used to create, produce, and deliver them.

→ Technology is an enabler of processes. When applied correctly, technology increases customer and operational value by improving the effectiveness and efficiency of your processes and the quality of your output. Great operations professionals know that they should never pursue a technology without first considering the processes that it will impact.

→ Processes can be grouped into three logical types: management processes, core processes, and support processes. Each must be defined, understood, learned, and managed effectively in order to achieve operations excellence.

→ For any of these processes to be effective, they must be managed with discipline. Business process management is achieved through five fundamental practices: process definition, standard operating procedures, process change management, process measurement, and quality assurance and control.

→ Operations leaders who are passionate about excellence know that simply upgrading established processes won't improve business or expand customer reach; they must search constantly for new and better ways to exceed customer expectations. These leaders know that to stay ahead of the competition, they must develop new products and services and expand their operational capabilities and capacity to deliver them.

→ Many executives find technology frustrating because (1) it is expensive, and (2) the asserted value of technologic investments is often difficult to realize. If you can accept five basic facts about technology and stick to a disciplined evaluation, acquisition, and implementation process, these frustrations can be minimized or eliminated.

Note: [1] Umble, Elizabeth J., and M. Michael Umble. "Avoiding ERP Implementation Failure." *Industrial Management*, January, 2002.

ACCOUNTABILITY:

Driving success and ensuring that the organization
is always moving toward its vision.

Accountability

Business Performance
Management

How is my operation doing? Is it on track to meet the company's goals and objectives? Is the company moving in the right direction to achieve its vision? To answer these questions, leaders must establish accountability by defining quantifiable metrics and measures. The development and oversight of these metrics is called *business performance management* (BPM).

BPM not only gives leaders and managers a tremendous advantage in managing day-to-day operations, it also illuminates performance trends invaluable to strategic business planning. Approaching BPM in a measured way allows you to oversee the effectiveness of your strategies, the impact of your initiatives, and the progress your organization is making in achieving its goals and objectives. As author and management consultant Peter Drucker once wrote, "You can't manage what you can't measure."[1]

You'll never achieve excellence without employing metrics and measures to drive accountability. However, establishing appropriate metrics can be a daunting task. According to a 2009 *Best Practices* report published by The Data Warehousing Institute,

> The wrong metrics can have unintended consequences: they can wreak havoc on organizational processes, demoralize employees, and undermine productivity and service levels. Metrics must accurately translate the company's strategy and goals into concrete actions that employees can take on a daily basis.[2]

Key Operating Measures

Metrics used to evaluate ongoing performance in functions related to critical customer requirements are called *key operating measures* (KOMs) or sometimes *key performance indicators* (KPIs). These measures serve as links between employees, processes, technologies, business results, customer requirements, and overall customer satisfaction and loyalty. KOMs inform us of our progress and performance in meeting goals and objectives and our customers' expectations. Some key points to remember about KOMs:

→ They should be based on customer requirements.

→ They must be tracked over time.

→ They should serve as catalysts for continuous improvement.

→ They should be tied to your key business drivers.

It is not enough simply to know how your company is doing; KOMs must be put to use. The purpose of metrics and measures is to provide performance data and information that can be synthesized into good business decisions. Questions that KOMs should answer include:

→ Are we meeting the expectations of our customers and stakeholders?

→ How do we grow revenue and increase our customer reach?

→ How can we improve customer satisfaction and loyalty?

→ How do our performance trends compare to those of our competition?

→ To what should we commit investment dollars and resources?

→ In which areas can we do better?

→ What value is our investment in technology delivering?

Whether directly or indirectly, each of your operation's KOMs should support your company's organizational, strategic, and operational goals. By developing and referencing appropriate, accountability-driven KOMs that align with your established goals, you'll be able to oversee and maintain accountability, guaranteeing that those goals are met. After they've been implemented long enough to produce valuable customer-focused data, KOMs will ensure that customer requirements are considered throughout the business planning process.

By crafting short- and long-term strategies around actual facts and data, you will experience greater success and fewer missteps!

Developing KOMs

The following six steps outline an iterative process that begins with the definition of high-level metrics and measures and ends with the development

Figure 6.1 Key Operating Measures Development Process

(metrics defined below are for example purposes)

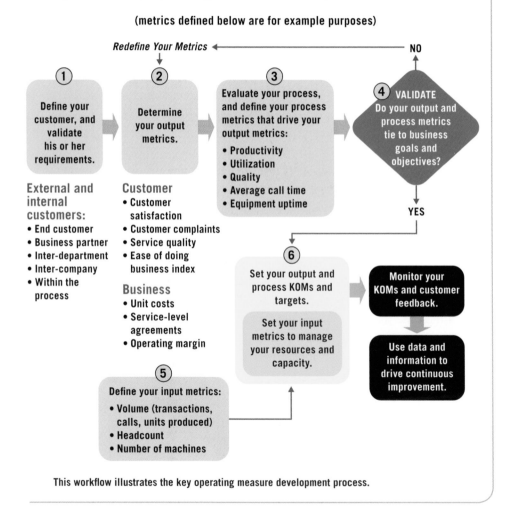

This workflow illustrates the key operating measure development process.

of a balanced scorecard (a process addressed in the following section). Although the development of KOMs is a relatively simple process, it requires a certain degree of thought and due diligence. Above all else, you must ensure that lower- and higher-level metrics align, and that your metrics help you manage your operation and serve your customers' expectations. Figure 6.1 on page 117 illustrates the six-step development of a KOM. Note in the figure that the fourth and fifth steps both flow into the sixth step; the process is sequential but not linear.

First, define your customers and ensure that you understand and can validate their requirements. Are your customers external, internal, or a combination of the two? Do you have the information and data needed to fulfill your customers' requirements? Do you have product specifications, well-defined service level agreements, and customer feedback in hand? Have you spoken to your customer directly? Developing a clear understanding of your customers and their requirements is the critical first step in defining your key operating measures.

Second, define your output metrics. Conduct brainstorming sessions with your leadership team to identify the few critical measures that will satisfy customer requirements and help your team manage and grow the business. Start small with 10 to 12 measures, and as you work through the defining process, group your measures into four categories: customer-focused measures, financial measures, operational (or internally focused) measures, and innovation and knowledge (or employee-focused) measures.

Third, evaluate your process and define the process metrics that drive the output metrics you developed in the second step. Process measures are typically internal operational or financial measures, and almost all high-level output measures will be driven by multiple metrics. For example, a customer satisfaction metric might be driven by call waiting time (hang time), call drop rate, product unit cost, and facility uptime. It is your and your leadership team's responsibility to decide which metrics are the most critical to the achievement of your customer satisfaction goals.

Fourth, validate that your output and process measures tie to your business goals and objectives.

You can do this in parallel with measure definition to minimize development time. If you cannot tie a measure to your goals, ask yourself, "Why are we measuring this?" Measures that do not pass this test should be reevaluated to determine whether they should be dropped, revised, or used as is. Once you have established the validity of a key operating measure, you're ready to start using it to manage your business, make adjustments to performance, and drive continuous improvement in your operation.

Fifth, define your input metrics. Input metrics such as volume and headcount are critically important to managing resources, capacity, and growth. They provide the information needed to gain a complete picture of how your business is doing. At what rate does headcount increase as volume increases—and why is this important? Are you able to maintain productivity, quality performance, and unit cost as volume fluctuates or headcount increases? If not, how do you correct the problem to meet your customers' requirements? These are all important questions that you cannot answer if you haven't defined output-related input metrics. Because a single input metric can influence multiple output metrics, the fifth step occurs outside of the expected flow of KOM development. Giving thoughtful consideration to input–output metric relationships provides the business intelligence needed to manage performance effectively.

Finally, set your output and process key operating measures, and establish your balanced scorecard. When establishing KOMs, you should establish a targeted level of performance that you want each KOM to help you achieve. If you've already established a performance baseline, set stretch goals rather than easily achievable targets that might be a slam dunk. **Don't resign your organization to sandbagging!** If you are new to metrics or do not already have a baseline from which to work, you should set goals that take work but are achievable. Your intent should be to motivate your employees, not demoralize them. Adjustments can always be made as you gather more performance data. Your initial scorecard will serve as the basis for annual business planning and the development of your operating plan.

The Balanced Scorecard Approach

Business performance management is most effective when employees at all levels of the organization are involved in its implementation. Employees should understand the reasons for and methodology of implementation, as well as the impact that BPM will have on them and on the business as a whole. Some may ask, "What does this mean to me?" or "How will this impact my position in the company?" It's your job to answer them—a task that is much easier if employees are engaged in the process. Even if your employees are all on board, the establishment of a successful performance management process can be a trying experience. However, if you follow the balanced scorecard approach, it doesn't have to be.

Robert S. Kaplan and David P. Norton's *The Balanced Scorecard* outlines a successful strategic approach to business performance measurement. This approach provides leaders and managers with the power to stay on top of business performance and take corrective action when performance falls below expected goals. By tying KOMs to business strategies, organizations can achieve their long-term strategic goals and ultimately, their visions. The key areas of measurement in the balanced scorecard approach are:

→ Customer: *How do our customers see us?*

→ Financial: *How do we look to our shareholders?*

→ Operational (the internal perspective): *What must we excel at?*

→ Organizational, or Innovation and Knowledge: *Can we continue to improve and create value?*

Figure 6.2 depicts a simple balanced scorecard. An executive team might use a scorecard such as this to monitor and manage the performance of its business. Reference this figure and the following guidelines when developing your own scorecard.

Figure 6.2 A Simple Balanced Scorecard

Operations Scorecard

Vision: Become the provider of choice for our customers by delivering innovative services and solutions that fulfill their processing needs

Customer	Financial
Drive customer value through innovative capabilities and services.	*Deliver positive financial results through strong financial management and ongoing continuous improvement.*

Customer			Financial		
	Goal	Status YTD		Goal	Status YTD
Customer Satisfaction	____	▇	Operating Expense vs. Budget	____	▇
New Customers	____	▇			
Customer Retention Percentage	____	▇	Total Headcount	____	▇
Self-Service Transactions as a Percentage of Total	____	▇	Revenue per Employee	____	▇
			Cost Reduction vs. Plan	____	▇

Operational	Innovation and Knowledge
Improve our processes and technologies to support the dynamic needs of our customers.	*Develop our employees and deliver new products and services to meet the needs of our customers.*

Operational			Innovation and Knowledge		
	Goal	Status YTD		Goal	Status YTD
Unit Cost	____	▇	Employee Satisfaction	____	▇
Productivity	____	▇	Employee Retention	____	▇
Quality—Percentage of Errors	____	▇	Number of New Products Released	____	▇
Expense per Employee	____	▇	Revenue from New Products	____	▇

1. The balanced scorecard is a one-page, executive-level snapshot. Depending on the size of your organization, each segment of the business might have its own scorecard.

2. Scorecards are comprised of five elements: a header that clearly states the company vision and a quadrant for each of the key areas of measurement.

3. Each key area is headed by a topical strategic objective or question to answer.

4. Specific metrics are listed below the strategic objectives of each key area. Quantitative goals are listed next to their respective metrics, and a color-coded status bar illustrates quickly your company's progress in achieving those goals.

5. Subsequent levels of detail about each metric can be appended so that leaders can drill down into specific information about individual measures.

Figure 6.3 illustrates appended information for the headcount metric. Appended information might include segmented measurements, additional data, diagrams, and any other indicators critical to managing a metric. Additional metrics that are unique to a particular business unit but might not necessarily fit on the top-level leadership scorecard should be appended. Trend graphs and charts should also be included to highlight changes in performance and draw attention to potential flags. This information should span every segment of the business unit so leadership can see how each segment is performing on its own and in conjunction with others.

Interlinked metrics work together to drive the success of your business strategies and move your organization toward its vision.

Figure 6.3 Appended Information for the Headcount Metric

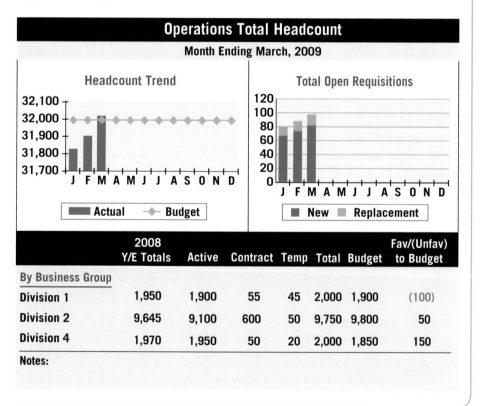

	2008 Y/E Totals	Active	Contract	Temp	Total	Budget	Fav/(Unfav) to Budget
By Business Group							
Division 1	1,950	1,900	55	45	2,000	1,900	(100)
Division 2	9,645	9,100	600	50	9,750	9,800	50
Division 4	1,970	1,950	50	20	2,000	1,850	150
Notes:							

Figure 6.4 depicts a sample *management by fact* (MBF) worksheet. Providing leaders with the answers they need to get failing metrics back on track and serving as a reference document of past pitfalls, the MBF is a concise and effective method of managing corrective actions taken in response to yellow- and red-coded metrics. Reference this figure and the following guidelines when developing your own MBF worksheet.

1. Trend charts highlight key performance indicators and how they are progressing.

2. Information about the problem's root cause is provided to demonstrate an understanding of why the metric is off target.

3. Brief corrective action information is provided to explain the steps taken to correct the problem.

4. The employee accountable for the corrective action is indicated, and a date by which the corrective action is to be completed is set.

Figure 6.4 A Sample Management By Fact Worksheet

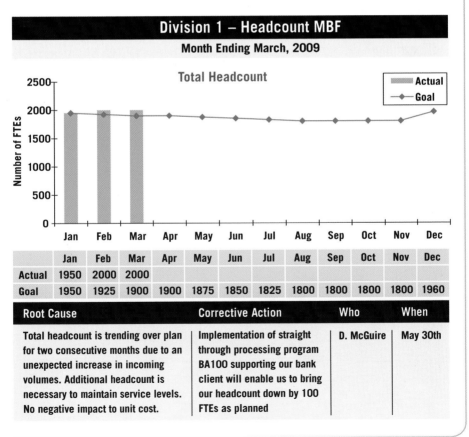

Division 1 – Headcount MBF
Month Ending March, 2009

Total Headcount

	Jan	Feb	Mar	Apr	May	Jun	Jul	Aug	Sep	Oct	Nov	Dec
Actual	1950	2000	2000									
Goal	1950	1925	1900	1900	1875	1850	1825	1800	1800	1800	1800	1960

Root Cause	Corrective Action	Who	When
Total headcount is trending over plan for two consecutive months due to an unexpected increase in incoming volumes. Additional headcount is necessary to maintain service levels. No negative impact to unit cost.	Implementation of straight through processing program BA100 supporting our bank client will enable us to bring our headcount down by 100 FTEs as planned	D. McGuire	May 30th

It is surprisingly easy to go overboard when developing metrics. Often leaders end up measuring things that are not really important. Sometimes, operations leaders measure things simply because they can access the data easily and they want to measure **something**. This defeats the purpose of key operating measures. As stated earlier, your KOMs should be tied to customer requirements, align with business strategies, and help you manage your business. Certain measures such as volume and headcount may not meet all of these requirements, but they are important inputs that must be measured to ensure the effective management of your resources overall.

When developing your KOMs, start small and **keep it simple!** (There's that phrase again.) You should begin by establishing two or three measures for each of the four key areas of measurement. Each of these areas will correspond to a quadrant of your balanced scorecard. Document each metric's definition, determine how it will be calculated, and establish the objective it will achieve or question it will answer. Once you have established a basic set of metrics and have tested it in actual practice for a number of months, you can go back and revise accordingly.

Whether because they get caught up in excessive metric definition or because they fear that they'll never get the data to support the measurement, some operation leaders get frustrated and give up. When developing your scorecard, don't worry about not having all the data. Focus first on

defining the metrics you need to manage your business and get them on your scorecard. You can figure out how to get the data later. Having the metric on your scorecard will provide the motivation to get the data. When you **are** ready to begin collecting data, your initial processes may be strictly manual efforts. It may sound archaic, but assigning interns or co-ops to gather information from machines, computer workstations, and employee worksheets is as good a place to start as any. Through trial and error, your people will develop novel ways of streamlining and automating the process. Engaged employees are very resourceful—you might be surprised by how quickly they can build a fully functional measurement system once the benefits of doing so become apparent.

The insights gained from implementing a metrics-based performance management system can be vast. Perhaps most amazingly, the benefits of implementation can be realized in a very short time if you follow the process step-by-step (Figure 6.5). How much money would a 15 percent improvement in operational performance free up in **your** business? If you have not

Figure 6.5 Developing a Successful BPM System

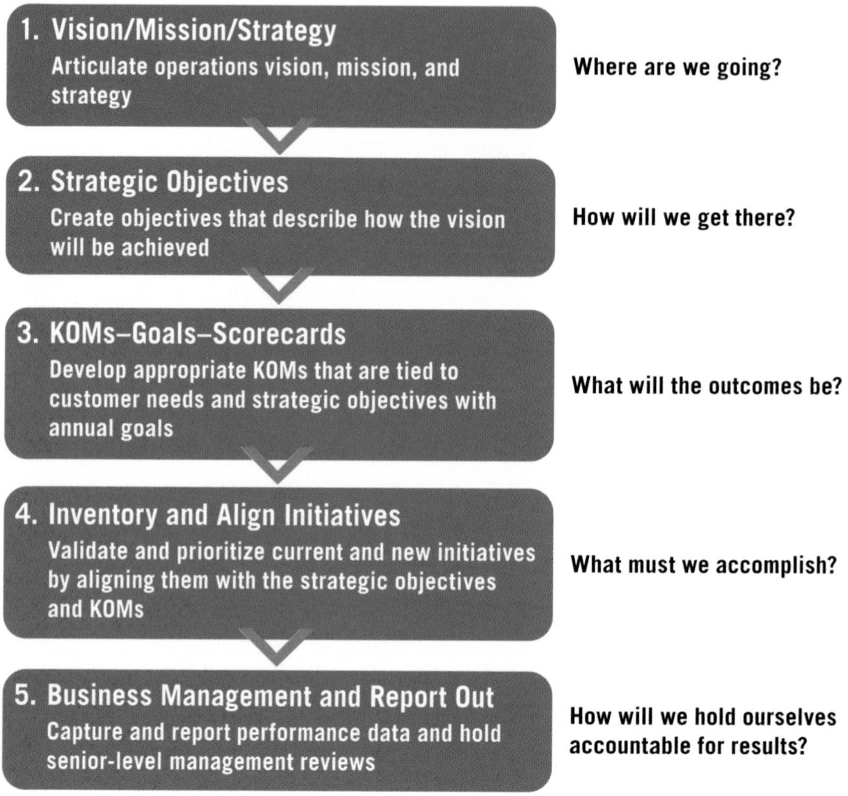

1. Vision/Mission/Strategy
Articulate operations vision, mission, and strategy

Where are we going?

2. Strategic Objectives
Create objectives that describe how the vision will be achieved

How will we get there?

3. KOMs–Goals–Scorecards
Develop appropriate KOMs that are tied to customer needs and strategic objectives with annual goals

What will the outcomes be?

4. Inventory and Align Initiatives
Validate and prioritize current and new initiatives by aligning them with the strategic objectives and KOMs

What must we accomplish?

5. Business Management and Report Out
Capture and report performance data and hold senior-level management reviews

How will we hold ourselves accountable for results?

The development of a BPM system mirrors the fundamental elements of operations excellence.

yet employed (or decided to employ) the balanced scorecard approach, you might consider reading Robert S. Kaplan and David P. Norton's *The Balanced Scorecard*. Its expanded exposition may provide better insight into the process, how it works, and how you can apply it in your own business.

Dashboards and Other Tools

The terms *scorecard* and *dashboard* are often used interchangeably in the business world, but there are definite differences. Scorecards provide senior management with a quick snapshot of how the business is doing, enabling managers to scrutinize specific details if necessary. Scorecards usually present KOM data at monthly intervals and can be used for formal operations reviews. Dashboards are typically used by front-line managers to monitor real-time performance data at individual and team levels. They may also exhibit critical process and machine data in real time, which enables managers to monitor processes and adjust quickly when performance deviates from specified limits. A performance management dashboard is much like that on a car. On the dashboard of your car there are a number of operational dials that provide you with information about the performance of your vehicle. Fuel levels, oil pressure, RPMs, speed, and temperature are all indicated visually. While these indicators tell you how your car is performing, they don't tell you where you're going or how close you are to getting there.

While both scorecards and dashboards are exceptional instruments, the specific tools and technologies used to manage your operational performance data and deliver management reports in a timely manner will vary. The components of your business performance management system will vary from those of your competitors and other operations in size, complexity, and cost. From simple programs developed by single-man shops to large enterprise solutions like IBM's Cognos Metrics Manager and MicroStrategy's BI Software, there are numerous *business intelligence* (BI) applications available today. As with any technology investment, you will have to decide what is best for your situation. At the beginning of your journey toward excellence, start small by establishing a manual data collection process for a few key metrics. Use basic software such as Microsoft's Excel and Access to oversee management reporting. Once you have the basics down pat, you can reevaluate and grow your efforts.

The use of metrics and measures, like the use of a performance scorecard, is common sense to operations professionals and can easily be applied to any business regardless of size or industry. Unfortunately, there are many businesses and operations that simply do not use them. Business performance information and data are powerful. They keep you on track toward your vision, provide tangible evidence as to whether your business strategies are working, enable you to correct your course quickly, and provide the intelligence you need to make decisions and plan strategies effectively. Without measurements, you're flying blindly—and quite possibly in the wrong direction.

Operational
Excellence
in Action

Accountability

Customers

Leadership

Process &
Technology

People

Life examples of leaders
like you.

Ian's
Industrial Parts

Old vs. New

IAN'S INDUSTRIAL PARTS HAS EXPERIENCED SOME MAJOR CHANGES during the last year or so. Adapting to the recession has altered customer relationships, employee work structures, and production processes. Externally, some competitors have gone out of business while others have emerged, and customers' needs and expectations have changed. These days, Ian barely recognizes the environment in which his company operates. However, amidst all those changes, business seems to be stabilizing. Industrial Parts has managed to stay both competitive and profitable, and the company's long-term outlook is good.

Despite a stabilized market, Ian knows that he must stay diligent in his efforts to continuously improve. He wants to stay ahead of the competition, and he knows that to do so he must be relentless in his pursuit of improvement. He is happy to see that his bottom line is improving, but he wonders if he can further impact quality, speed of delivery, and unit cost by reducing the lot sizes of his production runs. Currently, Ian is running a lot size of 100 for one of his new high-volume component parts. To minimize the cost of retooling and restructuring the work floor, his engineers used an existing process to build this new part. This allowed for an almost immediate shift in production, which allowed the company to meet customers' tight delivery requirements. Furthermore, it just made sense; when this process was implemented, running a lot size of 100 was the best and most cost-effective use of the company's capacity. The process is still effective and relatively efficient, but Ian believes that driving toward a lot size of one might significantly improve customer service and the overall profitability of the part. In the interim, a production analysis suggests that speeding throughput and producing the part in lots of 10 possesses a great deal of improvement potential. How can Ian determine whether this would be a good first step to take?

Solution:

Ian pulls his production team and key suppliers together to review the analysis and determine the best way to approach the challenge. They know that key operating measures will provide them with the information and data they need to make informed decisions and guide them as they make changes and improvements to the production process. They decide to remove 10 units at a time from the part's production run to gage the impact of smaller runs on the company's production processes, employees, suppliers, and customers. Keeping everyone in the loop throughout this end-to-end process will provide multiple perspectives and generate many good ideas, they conclude. Every time 10 units are removed from the lot, data and information generated

by the KOMs will highlight what needs to be done to make sure performance continues to move in a positive direction. Ian and his team use the following KOMs to guide them:

Set-Up Time: How long does it take to prepare each lot of parts for each step of the process?

Total Cycle Time: How long does it take to complete each lot of parts, as compared to the original lot size?

Defect rate: How many defective parts per million are detected at each control point as the number of units is gradually reduced?

Daily Production Volume: How many total units are produced each day, as compared to the original lot size, using the same number of people?

Unit Cost: Including both materials and labor, what is the average unit cost per part as the number of units is gradually reduced?

On-Time Delivery: How effectively can customers' delivery requirements be met in the quantities needed to support their demand?

Beth's Scorecard

OVERALL, BETH IS SATISFIED WITH THE WAY HER BAKERY AND STORE-FRONTS OPERATE. Business has been increasing steadily and her catering service has had a positive impact on her revenues and bottom line. To monitor her progress and business success, she focuses on three particular numbers each month: her revenue, expenses, and profit. This system has served Beth well, but now that her business is growing, she wants to identify opportunities for improvement on an ongoing basis and engage employees in the operation and expansion of the bakery. If her employees understand the impact they have on business growth and profitability, they will be better equipped to offer ideas and suggestions for further improvement. They will also be more active in day-to-day operations and have more opportunity to grow and develop alongside the business. How might Beth go about identifying opportunities for improvement and better engaging employees?

SOLUTION:

Beth realizes that her best option is to expand the number of metrics she uses to run the business. More metrics will both give her better insight into operational effectiveness and help her and her employees identify areas of improvement. First, she meets with her management team to discuss customers' needs regarding quality, service, and value. They then brainstorm appropriate strategies and measurements they can utilize to better serve customers' needs and manage the business. Using the balanced scorecard approach, they establish the following strategies and measures:

1. *Customer:* Create a first-class customer experience by offering value-add services that increase customer satisfaction and loyalty.
   - Customer Satisfaction
   - New Customers
   - Customer Retention
2. *Financial*: Improve profitability through strong financial management.
   - Total Revenue
   - Outstanding Debt
   - Sales per Employee
   - Operating Expenses per Employee
3. *Operational*: Use business process management to improve the efficiency and effectiveness of the bakery and storefront operations.
   - Productivity
   - Percent of Baked Goods Scrapped
   - Spoilage Percentage
4. *Innovation and Knowledge*: Leverage employee talent to create new products and services that both increase the customer base and drive customer loyalty.
   - New Catering Customers
   - Percentage of Revenue from Catering
   - Number of New Products/Services Introduced
   - Employee Satisfaction

Beth and her team agree they've made a good start. Although they don't currently have data to support all of these measures, they will implement simple methods to gather the data over the next 90 days so they can establish a baseline for each metric. After baselines are defined, they'll reconvene to review the baseline information and agree on the targets they want to achieve for each measurement.

Pioneer Processing → Leveling Out Performance

FELIX AND HIS OPERATIONS MANAGERS HAVE BEEN DOING AN EFFECTIVE JOB of providing quality service at a competitive cost to Pioneer Financial. With the new recognition technology scheduled for a fall implementation, he is excited about the opportunity to further improve PPS's processes and provide more value to the company.

While it has met great success, Felix's team has recently been challenged with a new problem: the number of employees needed fluctuates greatly on a daily basis. PPS receives an amazing amount of mail on Mondays (due to the weekend), but almost none on Fridays. Demand patterns reflect a marked increase in electronic transaction volumes on Tuesdays, followed by a sharp decline on Wednesdays. When marketing campaigns are launched, spikes occur in both mail and electronic volumes. Because Felix is not informed of new marketing campaigns, these spikes often take PPS by surprise. Felix's operations managers staff for peak volumes to maintain good service levels, but with the business growing and new technologies being implemented, Felix sees a tremendous opportunity to reduce expenses further. He knows that he just needs to manage PPS's daily employee count more effectively. How can he address this challenge?

Solution:

Felix and his operations team have two essential issues to address: (1) They need better communication with their internal customers, and (2) they must find a better way to manage daily staffing levels so they can increase capacity using the same number of employees as the business grows.

First, Felix and his operations managers meet with Pioneer Financial and Osprey marketing leaders. Together, they review PPS's quality, service, and cost performance data to validate that expectations are being met. Felix and his team highlight the improvement potential possible through better volume information, specifically as it relates to marketing campaigns. After discussing the end-to-end process and the impact that marketing's volume increases have on PPS, marketing's leadership agrees to provide operations a seat at the table when marketing campaigns are being planned.

Second, Felix's operations managers examine ways to match the number of employees needed to the actual daily demand. They know that staffing for peaks is unsustainable in the competitive financial market. Felix explains to his managers that if they expand their use of metrics and measures and establish a standard unit of labor for each of their primary transactions, they can track productivity and develop improvement initiatives to achieve a consistent level of productivity each day. They are daunted by the need to adjust headcount for peaks and valleys in demand, but he reassures them that new technology will provide detailed data to help them accomplish their goals. The result, Felix suggests, is a leveling of the number of employees needed each day. With volumes increasing, managers will actually be able to handle greater capacity with their current staff.

Because they are ahead of the actual technology implementation, Felix and his managers brainstorm the types of information and data they will need to more effectively manage the processing floor. Then, working with the technology group, they decide which data elements to collect: transaction type, transaction volumes by type, number of employees logged in, and actual time spent processing each transaction will be measured. Finally, by posting the daily volume and productivity numbers on the processing floor, Felix provides his managers and employees the performance data they need to see the effects their improvements are having on the leveling of performance and the achievement of productivity goals on a daily basis.

Trevor's Tech Reports → Boosting Subscription Rates

SINCE TREVOR BEGAN TECH REPORTS, much of the company's clientele has been generated by leveraging word-of-mouth recommendations and the network of contacts that Trevor and Teresa brought from their previous jobs. While he and his employees have been successful in establishing a reputation for providing reliable breaking information and sharp consultation, recent months have seen both subscription rates and consultation appointments begin to level off.

Trevor knows that in order to continue driving growth, he will need to develop new strategies and make new investments in his company's marketing efforts. He and Teresa have brainstormed a number of ideas, such as buying online advertising space, drafting informational mailers and brochures, attending and

creating detailed marketing strategies for conventions and conferences, and offering discounted consultation sessions and subscription rates.

He doesn't want to throw marketing dollars at just any idea that comes up. If he's going to make a serious investment in a new marketing campaign, Trevor wants to make sure that it will be effective. He decides that he needs to measure various marketing strategies' effectiveness—he needs to know exactly which marketing methods will spur the most site traffic and subscription growth, and how much they will do so. What methods could he use to do this?

SOLUTION:

Trevor's output metrics, site traffic, and new subscription rates are easy enough to measure using the analytics tools packaged with his web-hosting service and the data obtained from his subscription and consulting records. If he were to invest in online advertising, he could use online tools to monitor changes and patterns in site traffic. By keeping track of which advertising services and sites referred the most new visitors, Trevor could determine which ads were most effective. He could also monitor which and how many blog pages each new visitor viewed to determine whether he or she was just dropping in or had decided to explore the site in greater detail.

Trevor might also use various listening posts to obtain customer feedback about which marketing efforts were most effective. He could ask consulting clients to fill out surveys that asked how they heard about Tech Reports, why they did or did not visit the blog or subscribe to the newsletter, and whether they intended to schedule further consultation. Questions like these would help Trevor determine which advertising efforts were pulling the most traffic and new subscriptions. For example, by asking why clients decided to subscribe to the newsletter, he could get a better idea of whether advertising or subscriber discounts was more effective in capturing potential customers' attention and interests.

THE BUZZ

→ Approaching business performance management in a measured way allows you to oversee the effectiveness of your strategies, the impact of your initiatives, and the progress your organization is making in achieving its goals and objectives, and ultimately, its vision.

→ Key operating measures (KOMs) are metrics used to evaluate ongoing performance in functions related to critical customer requirements. These measures serve as links between employees, processes, technologies, business results, customer requirements, and overall customer satisfaction and loyalty.

→ KOMs serve as catalysts for continuous improvement. They should be based on customer requirements, tracked over time, and tied to your key business strategies.

→ Establish KOMs that align with your business's strategies, goals, and objectives. This provides you the ability to oversee and maintain accountability, which guarantees that your goals are met. KOMs that have been implemented long enough to produce valuable customer-focused data ensure that customer requirements are considered throughout the business planning process.

→ A balanced scorecard is a one-page, executive-level snapshot of five elements: a header that clearly states the company vision and a quadrant for each of the key areas of measurement (customer, financial, operational, and innovation and knowledge).

→ Distinct from scorecards, dashboards are typically used by front-line managers to monitor real-time performance data at individual and team levels. They may also exhibit critical process and machine data in real time, which enables managers to monitor processes and adjust quickly when performance deviates from specified limits.

→ When goals are not being met, leaders need to know how to put failing metrics back on track. The management by fact (MBF) worksheet is a concise and effective method of identifying and managing corrective actions taken in response to yellow- and red-coded metrics. MBFs also serve as good reference documents for past issues and challenges.

Notes: [1] Drucker, Peter F. *The Essential Drucker.* New York: HarperBusiness, 2001; [2] Eckerson, Wayne W. "Performance Management Strategies: How to Create and Deploy Effective Metrics." The Data Warehousing Institute. Accessed March 14, 2011. http://www.corda.com/pdfs/create-and-deploy-eckerson-jan09.pdf.

CONTINUOUS IMPROVEMENT:

A culture that facilitates operational effectiveness and enables the sustainable delivery of positive business results!

Continuous
Improvement

Finding Solutions that
Deliver Results

7

Expanding customer reach, growing the company, and increasing profitability are all indicators of a culture of continuous improvement. By developing such a culture, leaders can ensure that all employees remain actively engaged in and focused on meeting and exceeding customer expectations. The only way to develop a culture of continuous improvement is to be relentless in your pursuit of excellence and work on your business continuously and tirelessly. Great leaders are always on the lookout for opportunities to improve their businesses.

Continuous improvement must:

Be driven from the top down—It's about leadership!

Have aggressive stretch goals—It's about pushing your operation toward excellence!

Be process focused—It's about process, enabled by technology!

Be engaging and involve everyone—It's about people!

Deliver rapid change—It's about quickly demonstrating results!

Consider longer periods of implementation time for innovation and transformation—It's about sustainability!

Provide return on investment—It's about the bottom line!

Impact your operation positively—It's about results that drive your KOMs!

Utilize an effective communication process—It's about cohesion!

Provide a means to celebrate success and learn from failures— It's about development!

Manage risk—You can always go back to the old way!

One of the tools that you've already learned about, a performance management system that employs key operating measures and supports established business strategies, is an excellent tool for uncovering opportunities for growth. It ignites continuous improvement and acts as a compass for leadership, ensuring that the company stays on track to achieve its vision. The purpose of KOMs, after all, is to provide the performance data, trends, and information needed to **make good business decisions.** This chapter introduces a number of other highly effective tools and methodologies that you can implement to achieve an environment of continuous improvement, and ultimately operational excellence.

Developing a culture of continuous improvement promotes operational effectiveness and enables sustainable delivery of positive business results!

Where to Start

You might be thinking to yourself, "I want an environment of continuous improvement, but I don't know where to start!" You might be amazed by the opportunities that arise simply by establishing a solid foundation for sustainable improvement. Before you begin to embark on a new improvement program, ask yourself the following questions:

→ Are my core processes defined and documented?

→ Have I established quality assurance practices to monitor, manage, and build quality into my products, services, and processes?

→ Have I defined my key operating measures and instituted a balanced business performance management system?

→ Do I have the performance data, trends, and information needed to make good business decisions?

→ Do I have a baseline or measurable starting point from which to drive improvement?

If you haven't already, you should inaugurate your improvement efforts by putting these five basics in place. Remember: if your business is not built on a strong foundation of basic practices, every improvement effort you layer on top will eventually crumble.

Suppose an operations leader decides to overlook these fundamentals and instead initiates an improvement program right off the bat. Where should he or she start? If the leader thinks like most operations leaders, he or she knows that the logical starting point is the area of the business that is experiencing the most problems. Alternatively, the leader might hire consultants to help identify opportunities for improvement and initiate the program. Either of these routes will probably produce some degree of improvement in operations. **Unfortunately, neither will produce results that stick, and the leader will not sustain improvement over time.** After 12 to 18 months of implementation with limited measurable bottom line results, he or she will scrap the program and start all over again, wondering, "Why is it so hard to find a method that works? I'm focusing on my biggest problems and using the current best practices for improvement!" If you don't have a strong foundation in place, you'll never get to the root of your problems. Grasping at straws, you'll cure one symptom just in time for another to arise. You'll never be sure that you're working on the right thing or that you're really improving your business and moving toward your vision.

Improvement Programs

Operations build gradually. As a business grows and customer expectations change, the operation must grow and increase its capabilities and services to meet or exceed customer desires. This means that inefficiencies and waste such as redundant paperwork, overlapping processes, missing processes, and processes that are inefficient but stable enough to "get the job done" creep in. Bottlenecks, inefficient work-arounds, and other business-as-usual problems arise regularly in any organization experiencing growing pains. While these problems are often unavoidable and you will never reach *perfection* in your journey toward operations excellence, developing a culture of continuous improvement helps you get as close to perfection as possible.

Whether during a period of rapid growth or one of stability, you must follow an established improvement methodology to maximize results. For continuous improvement to be sustainable over time, a strong foundation must be in place as we discussed in the previous chapters. Figure 7.1 provides a logical progression for sustainable improvement to take hold and operations excellence to be achieved.

FIGURE 7.1 Continuous Improvement Solutions that Deliver Results

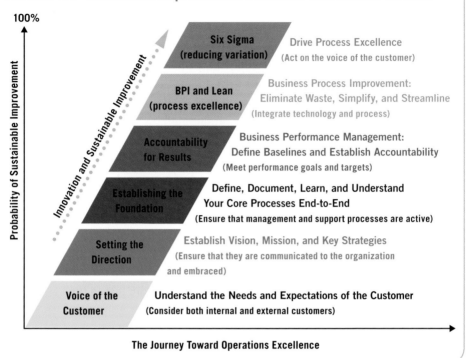

100%

Probability of Sustainable Improvement

Innovation and Sustainable Improvement

Six Sigma (reducing variation) — Drive Process Excellence (Act on the voice of the customer)

BPI and Lean (process excellence) — Business Process Improvement: Eliminate Waste, Simplify, and Streamline (Integrate technology and process)

Accountability for Results — Business Performance Management: Define Baselines and Establish Accountability (Meet performance goals and targets)

Establishing the Foundation — Define, Document, Learn, and Understand Your Core Processes End-to-End (Ensure that management and support processes are active)

Setting the Direction — Establish Vision, Mission, and Key Strategies (Ensure that they are communicated to the organization and embraced)

Voice of the Customer — Understand the Needs and Expectations of the Customer (Consider both internal and external customers)

The Journey Toward Operations Excellence

Understand that once the direction is set, improvement efforts begin while the foundation is being established. This is a fluid process. Quick hit improvements identified during this phase enable rapid, positive results that will energize and engage employees as they quickly see the impact their improvement efforts have on the operation, its employees, and their customers. Engaged employees serve as the springboard for a journey towards excellence. In the following sections, three well-known and effective improvement methods are outlined and compared. You may notice some similarities. When you decide to employ one of these processes, you must instill in your employees the discipline necessary to implement and stick to it. Constancy of purpose makes all the difference. When any of these three processes are married with a robust business performance management system and a companywide understanding of personal accountability, your results will absolutely shine.

Business Process Improvement

Business Process Improvement (BPI) is a simple and effective way to improve any business process at any level of your operation. It can reduce waste and bolster efficiency, delivering the maximum financial benefit to any business. By following a series of six interlinked steps, a BPI team can reveal and repair specific points of weakness within your processes. See Figure 7.2 on the next page. As with other continuous improvement systems, the six steps of BPI emphasize customers, measurement, planning, and execution.

1. **Understand the customer.** Listen to both internal and external customers! Determine whether the process is doing its part to meet their needs and expectations, and if it isn't, determine why and in which ways.

2. **Understand the process.** Document the workflow. Segment the process's individual steps, and chart each one. Determine the appropriate measurements to track performance before, during, and after changes are made. This documentation allows you to validate the effects of every improvement effort.

3. **Assess the process.** The documented process flow should be analyzed to determine which steps add value and which do not. Determine how to eliminate nonvalue-added steps and how to consolidate redundant steps to smooth the workflow. Collect and analyze process performance data, and compare it to customer requirements. This data helps identify opportunities for improvement. The BPI team should then devise strategies for improvement.

4. **Improve the process.** Some processes need adjustment; others may need radical reengineering. The BPI team must weigh the benefits of the improvement strategies and select the approach that is best for the business. The objective is to drive waste out of the process.

5. **Pilot the improved process.** Run a pilot test of the proposed improvement. Does it work as it should in the pilot project? Does it deliver the benefits projected?

6. **Implement, monitor, and continuously improve the process.** Create a rollout plan, train all affected employees, assess the results, and continue to make adjustments as necessary.

BPI may sound similar to cutting-edge improvement processes such as Lean and Six Sigma (both of which will be addressed shortly), but the BPI process actually provides a business improvement framework within which Lean and Six Sigma can be used.

Upon completing the assessment phase, operations leaders should have the basic information they need to determine whether Lean and/or Six Sigma are applicable. Through the voice of the customer, industry trends, and competitive threats, the effective use of BPI can point operations in the right direction, prompting radical re-engineering and innovation to leapfrog the

FIGURE 7.2 Business Process Improvement

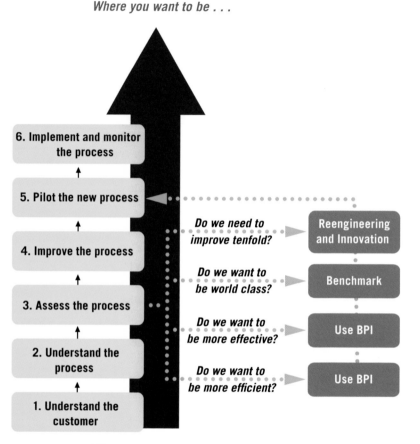

This diagram illustrates the six steps of Business Process Improvement.

competition. Bottom line, BPI provides a disciplined approach to driving operational change.

Lean

Between the late 1940s and 1975, Japanese manufacturing leaders Taiichi Ohno, Shigeo Shingo, and Eiji Toyoda developed the Toyota Production System (TPS), a continuous improvement methodology that championed the elimination of waste—*muda*, in Japanese—from operational processes. Toyota's groundbreaking system drew heavily on the teachings of W. Edward

Deming and Henry Ford's automobile manufacturing process. Originally called *just-in-time manufacturing*, TPS paved the way for the incredibly effective modern methodology called *Lean.* Lean, sometimes referred to as *continuous flow processing*, is a team-based, end-to-end approach to process optimization that systematically reduces waste by **relentlessly seeking out and eliminating** activities that do not create value for customers. Typical outcomes are characterized by minimized cycle times, optimized touch times, and continuous processing flows. The top seven wastes that Lean identifies and eliminates are:

1. Overproduction
2. Wasted time
3. Transportation
4. Process inefficiency
5. Unnecessary materials on hand
6. Unnecessary motion
7. Defective goods

By eliminating waste, your overall cycle time and cost of designing, ordering, manufacturing, and delivering the product or service are minimized, maximizing your bottom line. Like BPI, **Lean has six steps.**

Step One: Process or Line Analysis Create a process map or value stream map of your current process. In order to address every aspect of the supply chain, your map should extend beyond the four walls of the operation. It should also include suppliers and end customers. Every action required to design, order, and produce a specific product should be identified. After you create a process map, you should collect and document data to establish a baseline from which improvements can be made. Examples of the types of data to collect include:

→ Raw materials on hand

→ Number of transactions in queue

→ Processing and production time

→ Throughput rates

→ Finished goods on hand

→ Units produced per associate

→ Space utilized

Process analysis may begin within the four walls of the operation, but should expand as internal waste is eliminated and external waste becomes an evident priority due to the potential benefit to the business.

At this point, if you are not in manufacturing, you may not see the immediate benefit of Lean. You may even be tempted to skim the following few pages. **It's in your best interest not to!** Although Lean was designed for manufacturing, it can be applied to any industry or business process. Use of Lean concepts has snowballed over the last five years in the financial service industry as more and more companies realize the value of the methodology. The Executive Board Financial Services Operation Council's 2006 research study found that at least 40 percent of operational expenses resulted from wasteful activities that added no value for the customer. Institutions leveraging Lean techniques reported immediate results of 20 to 40 percent cost reduction in fewer than 18 months.

Step Two: Operational Improvement The process steps mapped out in step one should be sorted into three categories:

1. Those that actually create value (as perceived by the customer)

2. Those that create no value, but are currently necessary to product development, order filling, or production systems, and therefore cannot be eliminated immediately

3. Those that create no value (as perceived by the customer) and can be eliminated immediately

Action should be taken immediately to eliminate as many nonvalue-added steps as possible. This will streamline your processes, deliver rapid improvement, and encourage your employees to engage in the improvement process. The fruit of your employees' labors will inspire them and others in your operation to strive for bigger and more significant improvements. Once employees are engaged, improvement becomes contagious.

Step Three: Process Improvement

Once you have eliminated the nonvalue-added steps, use your map to identify less obvious opportunities to reduce or eliminate waste. Take a systematic approach, and group opportunities into categories. As you work your way through your organization's end-to-end process by identifying and grouping opportunities, you'll build a roadmap for implementation. Use that roadmap to improve your processes in a calculated, intentional way.

There are many approaches to process improvement. Some focus on short-term opportunities while others focus on long-term ones. Some start with the most difficult task, while others start with the easiest. Still others start by deciding how best to leverage their technology resources. One of the most impressive approaches to process improvement was developed by American consulting firm The Lab. The Lab's disciplined methodology is well documented and adhered to religiously. It yields tangible results quickly and consistently with a positive return on investment. You may be surprised to learn, however, that The Lab's methodology does not utilize advanced technology. In fact, it doesn't utilize **any** technology at all! Whatever approach you decide to take, keep one thing in mind: **your goal is to eliminate waste thoroughly!**

If you're inspired to follow The Lab's example, some strategies to reduce or eliminate waste without using technology are to:

→ Reduce transportation and travel time. In back-office operations, walk time is travel time.

→ Improve the workstation layout to eliminate excessive and unnecessary motion.

→ Minimize lot or batch sizes. Drive toward a batch size of one!

→ Eliminate idle time for both processes and employees.

→ Reduce pauses in operations and fluctuations in resource requirements.

→ Examine and eliminate rework loops.

When well-known improvement programs such as Six Sigma (which you'll read about shortly) are implemented without defined processes or a foundation of metrics, measures, and a management scorecard, the program is destined to fail. Why? Any improvement effort that is initiated without even this **minimal** foundation will create a veil of obscurity that forces management to ask itself, **"Is this really working?"** Such haphazard implementation goes against the very principles of Six Sigma, which bases improvement and increased customer satisfaction and loyalty on facts and data.

→ Stabilize unevenness in the delivery of work items and in the delivery process itself.

→ Implement flexible work hours to align resource levels with work volumes.

Step Four: Setup Reduction Preparing equipment, workstations, and other materials for use is a significant area of waste. Setting up your operation in a minimal timeframe is important not only because it improves efficiency but also because it allows for increased equipment flexibility. *Single minute exchange of die* (SMED) is a commonly used setup reduction process that can help you reduce your operations setup time by up to 90 percent. Investigation and implementation of SMED is highly recommended.

Step Five: Quality at the Source By reducing and ultimately extinguishing defects, you can ensure premium quality for the next customer in the process chain. If quality is the responsibility of everyone involved in a process, defective products and services will not escape from one process to another. While flaws in quality might not be apparent in the goods and services that come in, it must be designed into the goods and services that go out. **That's quality through prevention!** If every process operates under this banner, the waste of defective products will drop significantly.

Step Six: Pull-Based, Demand-Driven Operation Your entire process should be critiqued in terms of process flow to establish a pull-based production routine. By aligning production with actual customer demand, you can maximize efficiency and produce only what is needed to support customer orders. By using visual management instead of paper-based schedules, you can adjust material orders quickly and flexibly to sustain a production process based on actual demand.

Lean's Strong Points Lean differs from other continuous improvement methodologies in several ways. It focuses first on improving the process organically—that is, without technology. A tremendous amount of improvement can be realized by streamlining, simplifying, and standardizing your processes. Technology comes into the picture only after base improvements have been accomplished and the process has been optimized. The goal of most improvement methods is to develop work processes that are efficient, effective, and flexible, but unlike other approaches, Lean accomplishes this almost exclusively by reducing waste. Eliminating wastes associated with storage buffers, inspections, hand-offs, and nonvalue-added activities and operations such as administrative tasks is a hallmark of Lean. One of the best books on Lean focuses on the Toyota Production System. Edited by Japan Management Association and translated by David J. Lu, the recently reprinted *Kanban Just-In-Time at Toyota* is a simple but powerful classic. At only 184 pages, this book is packed full of Lean fundamentals.

Lean's Weak Points While Lean is a great method for solving problems, some operations professionals argue that it does not employ all of the advanced techniques that are needed to reduce process variation, such as statistical process controls, process capability (Cp/Cpk), and Failure Mode Effects Analysis (FMEA). When continuous improvement is focused on reducing process variation, especially in manufacturing or material processing environments, Six Sigma provides a disciplined methodology and a more advanced set of tools to drive process excellence.

DMAIC: The Six Sigma Approach

The final continuous improvement methodology of note is routinely employed by Six Sigma practitioners. Originating at Motorola, Six Sigma has been employed at businesses of all sizes for about 20 years. Like many improvement methodologies that came before it, Six Sigma has evolved into a comprehensive strategic approach to business excellence. Understanding the basics of Six Sigma is critically important to it successful implementation.

The approach has three primary areas of focus:

1. **Improving customer satisfaction**
2. **Reducing cycle time**
3. **Reducing defects**

Six Sigma uses facts and data to drive the development of solutions to business and process problems. In *What Is Six Sigma?* Peter Pande and Larry Holpp explain, "Six Sigma is a total management commitment and philosophy of excellence, customer focus, process improvement, and the rule of measurement rather than gut feel."[1] Sounds a lot like the basics of operations excellence, doesn't it?

Reaching a level of *Six Sigma* means that a business's process or products will perform with almost no defects: only 3.4 defective parts per million are allowed, to be exact. Understand this: if you do not have the basics of operations excellence in place, the probability of successfully deploying a Six Sigma strategy that provides lasting improvement is extremely low.

Using a disciplined, systematic approach to the identification and solution of work-related problems, Six Sigma's DMAIC process provides its practitioners with a common framework and language for process improvement.

D = Define the problem

M = Measure the process

A = Analyze the problem and measurement data

I = Improve the process

C = Control the new process

By focusing on the roots of problems, DMAIC practitioners aim not merely to treat symptoms but to extinguish issues entirely. DMAIC can

POINTERS

While leading Fidelity Wide Processing, operations leaders used DMAIC to improve our inbound and outbound processing operations. In 2002, inspired by the program's success, I challenged the organization to compete for the Association for Quality and Participation (AQP) National Team Excellence Award. Once again, we used DMAIC to maximize excellence and improve quality, service, and costs (to the delight of our customers)! Not only did we win the Team Excellence Gold Award in 2003 as a first-time competitor, we won the International Team Excellence Gold Award in 2004, becoming the first company ever to win back-to-back Gold Awards in the history of the program.

address improvement projects that have quick and obvious solutions (short-cycle problems) as well as those that are recursive, complex, or require detailed research (full-cycle problems). The level of detail and analysis needed for problem resolution varies depending on the situation. Using this process, you can remove barriers to effectiveness while encouraging an efficient, productive, and engaged workforce. See Figure 7.3.

Beyond DMAIC, the Six Sigma continuous improvement system employs numerous statistical tools for detailed problem analysis. While these tools all have their respective places and can be very useful under the right circumstances, their scope reaches far beyond the basics. All too often

FIGURE 7.3 The DMAIC Model

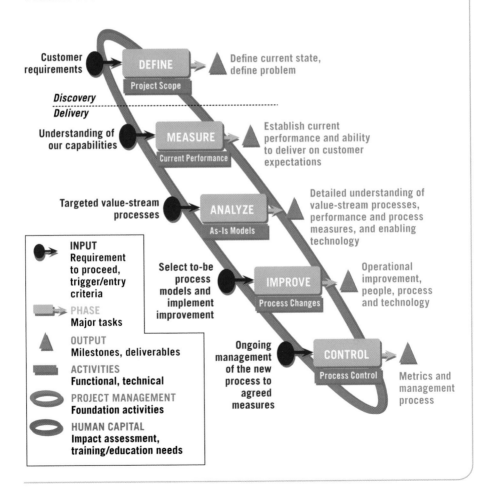

companies go overboard when implementing Six Sigma. They spend millions of dollars on programs that do not deliver positive financial results. Six Sigma's DMAIC is an extremely effective process for attacking most operational problems. It provides a disciplined approach that, when followed, yields positive results. However, it's very easy to overreach with Six Sigma, especially when the methodology is not fully understood, there is lack of clarity in its intent, and/or it is deployed haphazardly. It's important to understand which tools to use and when. Whereas the Lean methodology and the DMAIC process itself are relatively easy to learn, certain tools in the Six Sigma toolbox require extensive training and practice applying them in real-world situations. When using Six Sigma, be pragmatic and keep it as simple as possible. For an insightful executive summary and overview of Six Sigma, you should read *What Is Six Sigma?* by Pande and Holpp. It's an excellent resource for anyone interested in pursuing Six Sigma to improve her or his business.

From an actual practitioner's point of view, **real, tangible improvement is achievable through any improvement process provided there is discipline in its execution and accountability for results!** Whichever improvement process you choose, integration with the business's operating measures is key. For an in-depth review of the process improvement methodologies covered throughout this chapter, you are strongly encouraged to read *Juran's Quality Handbook* by Joseph M. Juran and Joseph A. De Feo.

Managers of a highly regarded revenue-generating unit at a leading financial services firm decided to initiate a Six Sigma program. Significant amounts of resources and investment dollars were committed to the program, and an expensive new website was created to highlight the unit and the work it was doing. After two years of implementation, the unit had trained numerous people in the ways of Six Sigma. A list of new projects, accomplishments, white papers, and other documents posted to the website touted great results, but there was one thing missing: **there was no real bottom line impact**. What was the reason that Six Sigma implementation ultimately failed for this dedicated and productive unit? It didn't track metrics or measures. Because KOMs were not tied to business strategies or used to manage the operation, the unit had no baseline from which to measure its improvement. The Six Sigma initiatives provided the appearance of improvement, but there were no tangible positive results. **Without measurable accountability, everyone feels good but nothing really improves—even with Six Sigma!**

THE BUZZ

→ Great leaders are always on the lookout for opportunities to improve their businesses. A performance management system ignites continuous improvement and acts as a compass for leadership, ensuring that the company stays on track to achieve its vision.

→ Business Process Improvement is a simple and effective way to improve any business process at any level of your operation. A BPI team can reveal and repair specific points of weakness by understanding the customer, understanding the process, assessing the process, improving the process, piloting the improved process, and implementing, monitoring, and continuously improving the process.

→ Lean is a team-based, end-to-end approach to process optimization that systematically reduces waste by relentlessly seeking out and eliminating activities that do not create value for customers. Lean has six steps: process or line analysis, operational improvement, process improvement, setup reduction, quality at the source, and pull-based, demand-driven operation.

→ Six Sigma uses facts and data to drive the development of solutions to business and process problems. The approach has three primary areas of focus: improving customer satisfaction, reducing cycle time, and reducing defects. By focusing on the roots of problems, DMAIC practitioners aim not merely to treat symptoms but also to extinguish problem issues entirely.

→ A culture of continuous and sustainable improvement is nurtured when an improvement process such as BPI, Lean, or DMAIC is married with a robust business performance management system and a company-wide understanding of personal accountability.

Note: [1] Pande, Pete, and Larry Holpp. *What Is Six Sigma?* New York: McGraw-Hill, 2001.

CONCLUSIONS:

Application of the fundamentals of operations excellence
deliver outstanding and sustainable results!

Conclusions

8

From the perspective of a practitioner who has achieved operations excellence in three industries, the topics covered in the first seven chapters of this book form the foundation for building an exceptional operation. Excellence is not rocket science—it's not even difficult—but without the fundamentals in mind, it's impossible to achieve. Excellence requires a disciplined approach in which success, failure, and progress along the journey are monitored and measured carefully.

Excellence begins and ends with leadership. Leadership must harness the talent and power of people to develop processes, which deliver exceptional customer value when enabled by value-add technologies. Courageous and effective leaders are not afraid to make tough choices, stand by unpopular decisions, or do what is right for their customers, their employees, and their businesses.

Leaders must be relentless in their pursuit of excellence!

In the words of legendary Green Bay Packers coach Vince Lombardi, "I would say that the quality of each man's life is the full measure of that man's personal commitment to excellence and to victory, whether it be football, whether it be business, whether it be politics or government."[1] This sentiment applies to you as an individual as well as to the business or operation you own or lead. To become the best of the best, you must be unremitting in your pursuit of excellence.

What can a leader such as you expect to achieve by focusing on the fundamentals? Well, the proof is in the results. This chapter is devoted to the marked improvements in performance, quality, service, employee engagement, and customer satisfaction that occur when a company decides to devote itself to a journey toward excellence.

Two Shining Examples of Operations Excellence

Pioneer Processing is a shared service utility within Pioneer Financial that provides both inbound and outbound processing services for Pioneer's five business units. Not unlike many large financial processing operations, Pioneer Processing receives new account requests and deposit notices (both by mail and electronically) and processes them through its centralized operation using imaging, character recognition, and check-scanning technology. On the outbound side, Pioneer Processing prints, assembles, and delivers monthly and annual customer statements and assembles and ships all literature requests for Pioneer product and service information.

Figure 8.1 illustrates Pioneer Processing's employee mean satisfaction scores over a five-year period and Figure 8.2 illustrates its employee engagement scores as calculated by Pioneer Financial's management effectiveness review process. These scores correlate directly with Pioneer Processing's

FIGURE 8.1 Employee Mean Satisfaction Scores

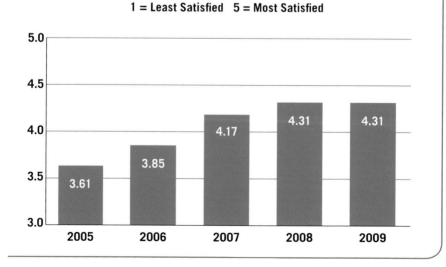

1 = Least Satisfied   5 = Most Satisfied

internal performance results, demonstrating that a truly engaged workforce is the driving force behind the achievement of sustained improvement—and ultimately—operations excellence.

Over 12 million literature requests and roughly one billion printed pages assembled into over 250 million envelopes were processed on an annual basis at Pioneer Processing. Figure 8.3 on page 156 illustrates four key quality measures used by Pioneer Processing's outbound operation to track the effectiveness of these processes. On-time delivery percentage is represented in both graphs as bars, and defective parts per million (PPM) is represented in both graphs as yellow lines. As the four measures indicate, a large volume of documents were processed on time and with defect rates that many times outpaced a Six Sigma level of performance.

Over 24 million pages of incoming documents and six million customer checks were imaged and electronically processed annually at Pioneer. Because documents had to be processed the same day, internal accuracy and on-time delivery goals were established to ensure that the majority of transactions would be in the hands of processing employees no later than 3:00 p.m. Figure 8.4 on page 157 illustrates two key quality measures used by Pioneer Processing's inbound operation to gage how well these goals were met. You may notice that the timeliness of imaging fluctuated slightly over time. This is attributable to the steep learning curve created by each year's large number of new customer implementations. As Figure 8.4 indicates, internal customer expectations were still consistently exceeded. To the delight

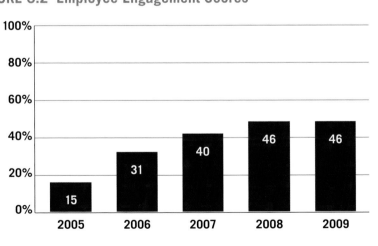

FIGURE 8.2 Employee Engagement Scores

FIGURE 8.3 Outbound Quality Measures

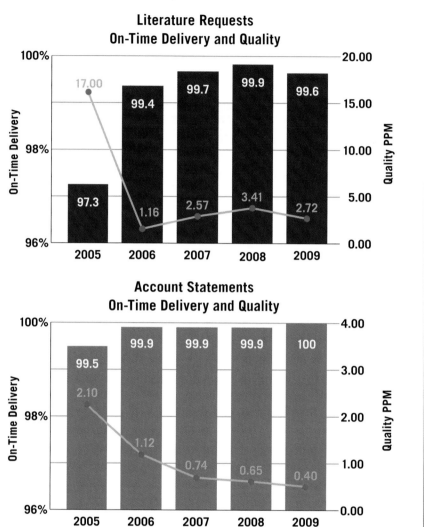

Literature Requests
On-Time Delivery and Quality

Account Statements
On-Time Delivery and Quality

of the business units that Pioneer Processing supported, the indexed unit cost of inbound transaction processing declined as Pioneer pursued continuous improvement (see Figure 8.5 on page 158). This was a true testament to employees' commitment to customer satisfaction and loyalty, and evidence of the continuous improvement culture they had created.

Focusing on three key metrics—volume, headcount, and expense—helped Pioneer Processing manage both its costs and the financial expectations of the business units it supported. By trending these three important

FIGURE 8.4 Inbound Quality Measures

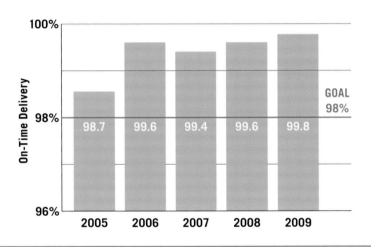

Transaction Processing Quality
(First Time Accuracy)

Accuracy

- 100%
- GOAL 99%
- 98%
- 96%

- 98.50 (2005)
- 99.00 (2006)
- 99.84 (2007)
- 99.87 (2008)
- 99.95 (2009)

Imaging On-Time Delivery

On-Time Delivery

- 100%
- 98%
- 96%

GOAL 98%

- 98.7 (2005)
- 99.6 (2006)
- 99.4 (2007)
- 99.6 (2008)
- 99.8 (2009)

metrics, Pioneer was able to validate its ongoing commitment to remain competitive, manage its resources, and provide real value to its customers (see Figure 8.6 on page 158). Pioneer Processing employees were relentless in their search for new ways to improve the business. They found original and innovative ways to improve processes and reduce expenses, generating consistent bottom-line savings every year. For example, innovation and technology improvements driven by Pioneer's technology organization helped simplify and automate manual processes, increasing capacity while maintaining headcount at levels that fostered significant financial improvement (see Figure 8.7).

Pioneer Processing's journey toward operations excellence produced outstanding and sustainable results that delivered exceptional customer value. Even though Pioneer's customer satisfaction performance dipped in 2008, its measurement systems and customer listening posts enabled

FIGURE 8.5 Inbound Indexed Transaction Unit Cost

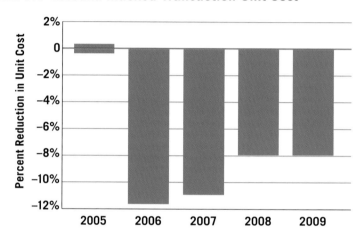

FIGURE 8.6 Volume–Expense–Headcount

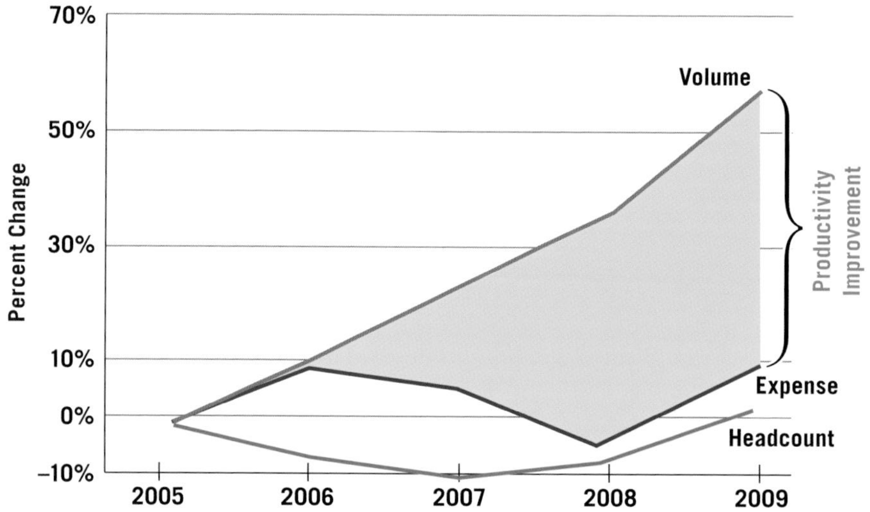

employees to identify the issues and respond quickly and accordingly (see Figure 8.8). **That's excellence at work!**

As a career-long student and practitioner of the employee engagement philosophy, I have had the privilege of working with exceptional people in numerous industries. Achieving double-digit improvements in quality and service and delivering millions of dollars in annual cost savings—all on

FIGURE 8.7 Recurring Annual Cost Savings

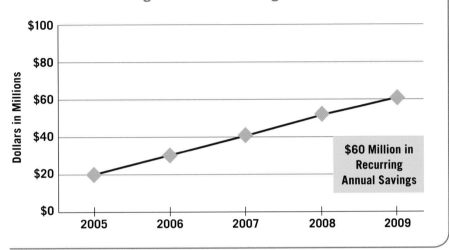

FIGURE 8.8 Historic View of Customer Satisfaction

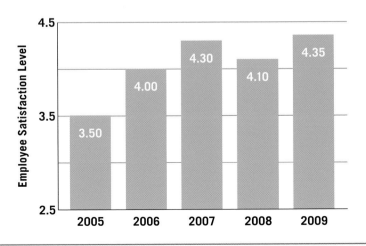

behalf of their customers—these extraordinary people have put their hearts and souls into their respective industries. Fidelity Wide Processing (FWP) was a shining example of an organization filled with such dedicated, engaged, and passionate people.

FWP was a business entity within the family of companies that make up Fidelity Investments, one of the world's largest providers of financial services. FWP facilitated high quality and cost-effective end-to-end customer communication through a full range of inbound and outbound services such as customer transaction and check processing, the production of personalized Fidelity literature, and the processing of monthly and quarterly statements. FWP's journey toward operations excellence was not a quick-fix solution or an overnight sensation. Like that of Pioneer, FWP's journey extended over multiple years of hard work and dedication. During that time, FWP's leadership team demonstrated a commitment to excellence that drove engagement scores upward, meeting a goal of four times as many engaged as disengaged employees. By focusing on management effectiveness and the basics of operations excellence, FWP experienced sustained operational success and consistent improvement in quality, service, cost, and customer satisfaction—all of which helped to establish FWP as a premier service provider within the Fidelity family of companies.

As Marcus Buckingham says in *The One Thing You Need to Know*, "Sustained success means making the greatest possible impact over the longest period of time."[2]

FWP's internal success was both highlighted and validated when it first competed for the Association for Quality and Participation (AQP) National Team Excellence Award in 2003. The AQP Team Excellence Award competition began in 1985 and has grown ever since, with over 800 teams participating so far. The award process promotes business excellence through a team-based approach. Winning teams are chosen based on how well they use their improvement process, rather than how much money they save. AQP says this helps to level the playing field and encourages more teams from more organizations to compete. It doesn't matter what improvement process the team uses, what matters is how well the selected process was used.

Needless to say, this competition was both challenging and very rewarding. FWP was up against 26 finalists: Analog Devices, Baxter Healthcare, Merrill Lynch, General Dynamics, ComEd, and five Boeing teams, to name a few. Though FWP had no expectation of winning as a rookie entrant, the team led by FWP director of quality Linda Nourse brought home the gold (Figure 8.9)!

FIGURE 8.9 Association for Quality and Participation (AQP) 2003 Gold Award Winner

Inbound Transaction Processing

Previous Work Flow

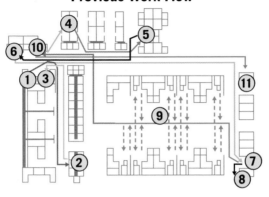

Work Flow Redesign

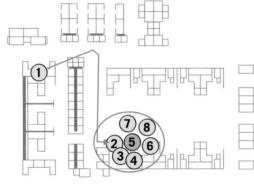

SOURCE: Bodinson, Glenn and Raymond Bunch. "AQP's National Team Excellence Award: Its Purpose, Value, and Process." *The Journal for Quality & Participation,* (Spring 2003): 37–42.

Team Project Results

→ **31%** improvement in **service delivery**

→ **33%** improvement in **productivity**

→ **32%** savings in **unit cost**

→ **60%** reduction in **customer reported defects**

→ **Estimated $1.9 million annualized savings!**

FWP's Incoming Customer Correspondence Process Improvement Team (*from left*): Chris Edgington, Mike Cook, Chris Hudac, Linda Nourse, Tom Duggan, Audrey Jett, Gregg Prebles, Paula Hays, Eric Carrol, Sue Divata.

FWP's second Gold Medal win in 2004 (Figure 8.10) was equally shocking. Although FWP was up against stiff competition including Analog Devices, Honda of America, JPMorgan Chase, Merrill Lynch, and ten Boeing teams (among others), the team was fired up about demonstrating true engagement and commitment to excellence. The team, once again led by Linda Nourse, did an outstanding job. They took home the AQP International Team Excellence Gold Award. **It was the first time a competitor ever received back-to-back AQP Gold Awards!**

The success stories of Pioneer Processing and FWP are but two examples of operations excellence at work—there are many more such stories tucked into the histories of exceptional companies and held in the hearts of their employees. If you seek out these organizations and employees, you'll find a common resonating theme: the basics of operations excellence.

As stated at the beginning of this book, the basics are fundamental—they do not change over time. The principles presented throughout this book are not new, and by now you surely have a good understanding of them. However, understanding and execution of the basics are two very different things. If you are committed to developing and leading an exceptional operation, ask yourself the following questions:

→ Do I know and understand our customers' expectations? Do my employees?

→ Do the foundational values of trust, respect, and integrity resonate in my business environment?

→ Have I as a leader established a vision for my organization and provided the clarity that my employees need to make that vision a reality?

→ Are the fundamentals of sound operations management in place?

→ Do my leadership and management teams actively hold themselves and their employees accountable for positive business results?

→ Do I hold myself accountable to do what is in the best interest of my customers, my employees, my business, and my community?

Your answers to these questions will provide you insight as to whether you're committed to operations excellence and the ongoing, sustainable delivery of exceptional business results. At a minimum, your responses should initiate a call to action for you and your organization to take the first steps in that direction. Or, maybe they'll help inform you of where you are in your journey. Either way, as a leader, don't lose sight of the basics—the fundamentals of operational success. They never change because they don't have to—they simply work.

FIGURE 8.10 Association for Quality and Participation (AQP) 2004 Gold Award Winner

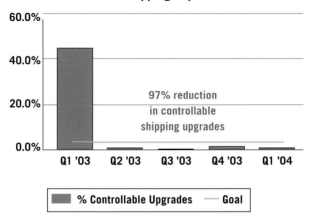

Bulk Shipping Improvement

97% reduction in controllable shipping upgrades

% Controllable Upgrades — Goal

Bulk Shipping Opportunity

78% of next-day shipments had been received in time to ship at discounted rate (indicating controllable costs)

Team Project Results

→ **44%** improvement in **bulk productivity**

→ **33%** improvement in **picking productivity**

→ **23%** improvement in **packing productivity**

→ **36%** reduction in **unit cost**

→ **97%** reduction in **controllable shipping upgrades**

SOURCE: Nourse, Linda and Paula Hays. "Fidelity Wide Processing Wins Team Excellence Award Competition." *The Journal for Quality & Participation,* (Summer 2004): 42–48.

FWP's Bulk Shipping Process Management Team (*from left, back*): David Gottman, Mike Cook, Howard Nemeroff, Brandi Lenihan, Kevin Lee, Linda Nourse, Donna Clancy, Paula Hays, Steve Wallace, Audrey Jett, Charles Goines, Tracey Bracke, Doug Sutton; (*front*): Alan Ramsey, Walter Jones.

THE BUZZ

→ Operations excellence means focusing strategically on maximizing the value that operations delivers to your customers. Through strong leadership, the power of people, the use of industry best practices, and the application of value-add technologies, operations excellence enables sustained delivery of high-quality, cost-effective services and capabilities that provide exceptional customer value.

→ Excellence begins and ends with leadership. Courageous and effective leaders are not afraid to make tough choices, stand by unpopular decisions, or do what is right for their customers, employees, and business.

→ Effective leaders provide organizational clarity and a credible vision of where they want the organization to go and how the company will get there. Effective leaders define outcomes, roles and responsibilities, and accountability for results.

→ The key to developing a high-performance work environment with employees who are truly engaged and committed to making a vision of excellence into reality is management effectiveness.

→ Processes are how we get things done. They must be defined, documented, understood, executed, and managed in a disciplined way to consistently meet or exceed customer requirements.

→ Technology should never be considered separate from process. It is an enabler of your processes and as such should be tightly integrated so that process and technology work together to drive positive business results and customer value.

→ For operations excellence to become a reality, accountability for results—that is, meeting the needs and expectations of our customers—is paramount.

→ Never lose sight of the basics. The fundamentals of operational success don't change over time because they don't have to—they simply work.

Notes: [1] Lombardi, Vince. *What It Takes to Be #1*. New York: McGraw-Hill, 2003; [2] Buckingham, Marcus. *The One Thing You Need to Know*. New York: Free Press, 2005.

Suggested Reading List

Beemer, C. Britt, and Robert L. Shook. *The Customer Rules*. New York: McGraw-Hill, 2008.

Buckingham, Marcus. *The One Thing You Need to Know*. New York: Free Press, 2005.

Buckingham, Marcus, and Curt Coffman. *First, Break All the Rules*. New York: Simon & Schuster, 1999.

Camp, Robert C. *Benchmarking: The Search for Industry Best Practices that Lead to Superior Performance*. Cambridge: Productivity Press, 1989.

Covey, Stephen. *The 7 Habits of Highly Effective People*. New York: Free Press, 2004.

Crosby, Philip B. *Quality Is Free*. New York: Signet, 1980.

Gabor, Andrea. *The Man Who Discovered Quality: How W. Edwards Deming Brought the Quality Revolution to America*. New York: Penguin, 1992.

Goldratt, Eliyahu M., and Jeff Cox. *The Goal: A Process of Ongoing Improvement*. Great Barrington: North River Press, 2004.

Ishikawa, Kaoru. *Guide to Quality Control*. Hong Kong: Nordica International, Ltd., 1982.

Japan Management Association, tr., *Kanban Just-In-Time at Toyota*. Cambridge: Productivity Press, 1989.

Juran, Joseph M., and Joseph A. De Feo. *Juran's Quality Handbook*. New York: McGraw-Hill Professional, 2010.

Kaplan, Robert S., and David P. Norton. *The Balanced Scorecard*. Boston: Harvard Business Press, 1996.

Lencioni, Patrick. *The Five Dysfunctions of a Team*. San Francisco: Jossey-Bass, Inc., 2002.

Lencioni, Patrick. *The Five Temptations of a CEO*. San Francisco: Jossey-Bass, Inc., 1998.

Lencioni, Patrick. *The Four Obsessions of an Extraordinary Executive*. San Francisco: Jossey-Bass, Inc., 2000.

Lencioni, Patrick. *Overcoming the Five Dysfunctions of a Team: A Field Guide for Leaders, Managers, and Facilitators*. San Francisco: Jossey-Bass, Inc., 2005.

Pande, Pete, and Larry Holpp. *What Is Six Sigma?* New York: McGraw-Hill, 2001.

Schiemann, William A., and John H. Lingle. *Bullseye! Hitting Your Strategic Targets through High-Impact Measurement*. New York: Free Press, 2005.

Smart, Bradford D. *Topgrading*. Paramus: Prentice Hall Press, 1999.

Walton, Mary. *The Deming Management Method*. New York: Perigree Books, 1986.

Index

Customer service, dedication
to, 4
Customer-supplier
relationship, 18–19
Customer surveys, 21

D

Dashboards, 126–27
Data, providing vital, 45
Decision making, employee
inputs in, 36
Deming, W. Edward, 46,
142–43
14-point management
method of, 46, 47
*The Deming Management
Method* (Walton), 47, 102
Discipline, 71–72
Divata, Sue, 161
DMAIC: The Six Sigma
Approach, 46, 140, 141,
147–50
DocuShare, 97
Double-digit improvement, 72
Duggan, Tom, 161
Duncan, Tim, 81

E

Edgington, Chris, 161
Eiji Toyoda, 142
EMC's Documentum, 97
Employees
building strong
relationships with, 46
commitment to, 4
as customers, 19
development of, as key to
high-performance work
environment, 64–66
engagement and
leadership, 57–59
evaluating performance
of, 46
safety and housekeeping
and, 69–74
as suppliers, 18–19
teamwork and, 75–81
Ennis, Mike, 68
Enron, 56
Enterprise Resource Planning
(ERP), 106
Entitlement, 64
Equipment demonstrations, 104

Excellence
characteristics evident in
environment of, 4
leadership and, 153
Expectations, exceeding,
22–23
External communication, 35
External customers, 17–18

F

Farmer, Scott, 69
Fidelity Brokerage Company,
17
Fidelity Employer Services
Company, 17
Fidelity Investments
Institutional Services, 17
Fidelity Retirement Services,
17
Fidelity Wide Processing
(FWP)
building strengths-
based organization
through management
effectiveness of, 160–63
goals and objectives of,
36–37
implementation of
Enterprise Resource
Planning system of, 107
investment in new mail
insertion equipment
of, 105
First, Break All the Rules
(Buckingham), 60, 61, 62
5S: The Five Pillars of a Safe
and Efficient Operation
(safety program), 70–74
*The Five Dysfunctions of a
Team* (Lencioni), 75, 77, 78
The Five Temptations of a CEO
(Lencioni), 12
Ford, Henry, 143
*The Four Obsessions of an
Extraordinary Executive*
(Lencioni), 35

G

General Dynamics, 160
Goals
leadership and, 42–44
using key strategies to
meet, 42–43

Goines, Charles, 163
Gottman, David, 163
Guide to Quality Control
(Ishikawa), 102

H

Hays, Paula, 161, 163
Healthy conflict in teamwork,
78–79
High-performance work
environment
creating, 58–59
teamwork in, 75–81
Holpp, Larry, 148, 150
Honda of America, 69, 162
Housekeeping, employees and,
69–74
Hudac, Chris, 161

I

IBM
Cognos Metrics Manager
of, 127
Websphere Business
Modeler of, 95
iGrafx's Process, 95
Implementation failure, causes
of, 106
Improvement programs,
139–50
Industrial Parts, 24–25
Information, providing vital, 45
Ingram, Ian, 24–25
Initiatives, key, 42–44
Innovation
technology and, 102–7
use of, 4
Input metrics, defining, 119
Institutional knowledge, 93
Institutional knowledge
syndrome, 93, 94
Integrity, 56–57
Interlinked metrics, 122
Internal customers, 17–18
"Investing in keeping the lights
on," 105
Ishikawa, Kaoru, 102

J

Japan Management
Association, 147
Jett, Audrey, 161, 163

About the Author

Doug Sutton is a hands-on operations professional and a proponent of the fundamentals of operations excellence. Doug developed his keen perspective and unique insights over 25 years in operations, during which time he served in a number of leadership positions and in multiple industries.

Doug began his career at Harris Corporation, RF Communications Group in Rochester, New York. There, he spent more than 10 years developing operations knowledge in the manufacture of high-frequency radio communication equipment for the United States Department of Defense and for developing countries. It was during this time that Doug first implemented the principles of Lean, process management, and metrics-based business performance management, earning him recognition for his skills in process engineering and operations management.

Doug was recruited to Bausch & Lomb's eyewear division in the summer of 1989. After spending four years developing a manufacturing center of excellence in Nuevo Laredo, Mexico, Doug served three years as the manager of engineering and operations at Bausch & Lomb's San Antonio sunglass fabrication, assembly, and distribution facility. While there, Doug worked with a hard-charging group of operations leaders to develop a manufacturing center of excellence, achieving ISO9002 certification.

Transitioning from manufacturing to financial services, Doug joined Fidelity Wide Processing, a division of Fidelity Investments, in 1997. It was here, with the aid of a very talented group of operations professionals, that Doug developed a complete understanding of the basics of operations excellence. With a clear vision and strategy, Doug and his colleagues successfully applied manufacturing concepts such as the Balanced Scorecard, Lean, 5S, and Six-Sigma to transform Fidelity Wide Processing into a world-class operation and premier service provider, winning back-to-back Gold Awards in the annual AQP National Team Excellence competition. In 2007, wanting to explore new challenges, Doug took an operations excellence leadership position in the insurance industry. After three years in the industry, Doug left to launch Operations Excellence Services LLC, a firm dedicated to helping business and operations leaders in their own journeys toward excellence.

Doug is a graduate of the Rochester Institute of Technology. A devoted family man and lover of the outdoors, Doug lives in Cincinnati with his wife of 28 years, Renee. They have three grown children: Ashley, Kyle, and Douglas. To learn more about Doug Sutton and Operations Excellence Services, visit **www.opexsvs.com**.